The FAITH of
Barack Obama

The FAITH of
Barack Obama

STEPHEN MANSFIELD

THOMAS NELSON
Since 1798

NASHVILLE DALLAS MEXICO CITY RIO DE JANEIRO BEIJING

Published in Nashville, Tennessee, by Thomas Nelson. Thomas Nelson is a trademark of Thomas Nelson, Inc.

Thomas Nelson, Inc., titles may be purchased in bulk for educational, business, fund-raising, or sales promotional use. For information, please e-mail SpecialMarkets@ThomasNelson.com.

Scripture quotations marked NIV are from the HOLY BIBLE: NEW INTERNATIONAL VERSION®. © 1973, 1978, 1984 by International Bible Society. Used by permission of Zondervan Publishing House. All rights reserved.

Scripture quotations marked KJV are from KING JAMES VERSION.

Page design: Walter Petrie

Library of Congress Cataloging-in-Publication Data

Mansfield, Stephen, 1958-
    The faith of Barack Obama / written by Stephen Mansfield.
        p. cm.
    Includes bibliographical references.
    ISBN 978-1-59555-250-1 (hardcover)
    1. Obama, Barack—Religion. 2. Presidential candidates—United States—
Biography. 3. Legislators—United States—Biography. 4. Religion and
politics—United States—Case studies. I. Title.
E901.1.O23M36 2008
328.73092—dc22
    [B]   2008023371

Printed in the United States of America

08 09 10 11 12 QW 5 4 3 2 1

To Beverly,
Song of my life

Contents

The Life of Barack Obama: A Chronology

1961   Born in Honolulu on August 4 to eighteen-year-old Ann Dunham and Barack Obama Sr., the first African student at the University of Hawaii

1964   Barack's parents divorced when he was two years old

1966   Ann married Lolo Soetoro

1967   Barack and his mother moved to Indonesia

1971   Returned to Honolulu and enrolled in Punahou School

      Ann and Lolo Soetoro divorced

1979   Entered Occidental University in Los Angeles

1981   Transferred to Columbia University in New York

1982   Barack Obama Sr. died in a car crash in Kenya at age fifty-two

1983   Graduated from Columbia University and went to work for Business International Corporation as a writer and analyst

1985   Began work with Developing Communities Project in Chicago

      Began attending Trinity United Church of Christ

1987   Lolo Soetoro, Barack's stepfather, died of a liver ailment in Indonesia

      Entered Harvard Law School at age twenty-seven

1990 Became the first African-American president of the Harvard Law Review

1991 Graduated from Harvard and returned to Chicago

1992 Married Michelle Robinson

Stanley Dunham, Barack's grandfather, died

1993 Began work with Miner, Barnhill & Galland law firm in Chicago

1995 *Dreams from My Father* was released, to light praise and attention

On November 7, Ann Dunham Soetoro died of ovarian cancer

1996 Elected to the Illinois State Senate from Hyde Park

2000 Lost a congressional primary race against incumbent Bobby Rush

2004 On July 27, made the Democratic Convention speech that launched him to national prominence

On November 2, won the Illinois general election for U.S. Senate

Dreams from My Father was rereleased to wide acclaim

2006 *The Audacity of Hope* was released and became a best seller

2007 On February 10, announced his candidacy for president of the United States

Introduction

IT WAS A COOL, OVERCAST TUESDAY IN JULY 2004, AND BARACK Obama was making the expected round of meetings before his speech that evening at the Democratic National Convention in Boston. He had come at the request of John Kerry, who upon meeting Obama knew that the young man might very well be the face of the Democratic Party's future. Kerry wanted Obama's story and thoughtful oratory to feature in the convention's symbolic pageant just then unfolding before the watching world.

That afternoon, Obama walked the Boston streets with his friend, Chicago businessman Martin Nesbitt. At each stop, eager crowds formed and pressed ever closer to the thin black state senator from Illinois.

"This is incredible!" Nesbitt gushed. "You're like a rock star!"

Turning to his friend, Obama replied, "If you think it's bad today, wait till tomorrow."

Nesbitt looked puzzled. "What do you mean?"

"My speech is pretty good," Obama explained. Clearly, he already had some sense of his destiny.[1]

That evening, after being introduced by Illinois senator Dick

Durbin as "a man who can help heal the divisions of our nation," Barack Obama strode to the rostrum to give the speech he was certain would resonate throughout the nation. Seventeen minutes later, he had decisively taken his place on the American political stage.

It was, by all accounts, the best speech of the convention, the kind that some politicians pray to give just once in their lifetimes. Though Obama did not shrink from extolling the superior heroism of John Kerry and the righteousness of Democratic Party values, he managed a tone that was somehow wise and apart. There was a nod to the limitations of government to solve problems, a call for an end to the political strife tearing at the nation's soul. Scripture and the poetry of the American experience surfaced gracefully, and all was infused with Obama's own story and what the promise of a "skinny kid with a funny name who believes that America has a place for him, too," might mean to others.

It was a masterful performance, and for those who listened to the speech with an ear for the overtones of faith, there was a single sentence that signaled a defining theme in Barack Obama's life. It came toward the end, at a moment when Obama criticized the pundits who divide the nation into red states, or those that lean conservative and Republican, and blue states, or those that tend to vote Democratic. At the beginning of a sweeping passage designed to reveal the folly of such labels, Obama exulted, "We worship an awesome God in the Blue States."

> "We worship an awesome God in the Blue States."

The sentence was nearly buried in the rhetorical flourishes

that followed. Though the words are but nine among more than two thousand, Obama intended them as a trumpet call of faith. No longer, he was saying, would the political fault lines in America fall between a religious Right and a secular Left. Instead, a Religious Left was finding its voice: *We, too, have faith,* they proclaimed. *Those of us on the political Left who believe in a woman's right to choose an abortion and who defend the rights of our gay friends and who care for the poor and who trust that big government can be a tool of righteousness—we also love God. We, too, have spiritual passion, and we believe that our vision for America arises from a vital faith as well. No longer will we be painted as the nonbelievers. No longer will we yield the spiritual high ground. The Religious Right has nothing on us anymore.*

It was a conscious attempt to reclaim the religious voice of the American political Left. Those nine words were meant to echo the footsteps of nuns and clergymen who marched with Martin Luther King Jr., of the religiously faithful who protested the Vietnam War or helped build the labor movement or prayed with César Chávez. Barack Obama was raising the banner of what he hopes will be the faith-based politics of a new generation, and he will carry that banner to whatever heights of power his God and the American people allow.

The faith that fuels this vision is fashioned from the hard-won truths of Obama's own spiritual journey. He was raised by grandparents who were religious skeptics and by a mother who took an anthropologist's approach to faith: religion is an important force in human history—understand it whether you make it your own or not. Nurtured as a child in the warm religious tolerance of the Hawaiian Islands and the multiculturalism of Indonesia in the late 1960s and early 1970s, he grew into a young man for whom race was more of a crisis than religion. As the son of a white American mother and a black African father who left the family when Barack was only two years old, he felt too white to be at home among his black friends, and too black to fit easily into the white world of his grandparents and mother. He was a man without country.

Ever the emotional expatriate, he was haunted by displacement through his college years and through his troubling experience as a community organizer in Chicago. It was not until he rooted himself in the soil of Trinity United Church of Christ on Chicago's South Side that he began to find healing for his loneliness and answers for his incomplete worldview. He experienced for the first time both connection to God and affirmation as a son of Africa. He would also be exposed to a passionate Afrocentric theology and a Christian mandate for social action that permanently shaped his politics. Through Trinity, he found the mystical country for which his soul had longed.

Yet he also found that through this country flowed a bitter stream. As he quickly came to understand, Trinity Church's broad Christianity was permeated by a defining, if understandable, spirit of anger: toward white America, toward a history of black suffering, and toward a U.S. government that consistently lived beneath the promise of her founding vision. If Obama himself refused to drink from this bitter stream, he was mentored by those who did. The senior pastor at Trinity, Dr. Jeremiah A. Wright Jr., had for decades given poetic voice to the anger of his people, and when his sermons reached the broader American public during the 2008 presidential campaign, it created the worst crisis of Obama's candidacy.

Still, besieged by critics from both the political Right and Left, Obama initially refused to abandon his pastor. Neither did he abandon his role as a champion of the Religious Left, and in this his timing was perfect, for the religious winds were just then shifting in American politics.

As the 2008 presidential campaign season unfolded, the Religious Right—the coalition of faith-based social conservatives that had defined the debate over religion in American politics for nearly three decades—was in disarray, if not decline. Jerry Falwell and D. James Kennedy, revered fathers of the movement, had recently died. Other leaders had been sidelined through scandal and folly. Ted Haggard, president of the influential National Association of Evangelicals, had fallen into disgrace through drug abuse and sexual immorality. Pat Robertson, once the leading voice of the Religious Right, had earned nationwide scorn when he called for the assassination of Venezuela's Hugo Chávez and then intimated that Israel's prime minister, Ariel Sharon, lay in a coma due to God's anger over Israeli "land for peace" policies. Clearly, the lions of the movement were passing from the scene, but a passing of the baton to a new generation of national leaders was nowhere in sight.

No longer unified and able to speak with one voice, the leaders of the Religious Right each went their own way in endorsing Republican candidates. Pat Robertson, long an antiabortion stalwart, endorsed Rudy Giuliani, the only pro-choice candidate among the Republicans. Bob Jones III, leader of the deeply fundamentalist Bob Jones University, endorsed the only Mormon candidate in the race, Mitt Romney. Longtime Religious Right kingmaker James Dobson issued statements attacking first Fred Thompson and then John McCain, only to endorse Mike Huckabee less than a month before the ex-governor dropped out of the race, much too late to have done any good. Strangely, few among the Religious Right seemed initially interested in Huckabee, a former Baptist preacher who spoke openly of his faith and extolled the virtues of faith-based politics. Of the remaining highly visible pastors in the nation, Joel Osteen and T. D. Jakes strained to remain nonpolitical, while Rick Warren and Bill Hybels went to great lengths to show that they were sensitive to and in some cases sympathetic with the priorities of the Religious Left, particularly as expressed by Barack Obama.

This fraying of the Religious Right was worsened by a surprising defection: evangelical voters, a mainstay of Republican politics for decades, began abandoning their party. By February 2008, esteemed pollster and cultural analyst George Barna was reporting that "if the election were held today, most born again voters would select the Democratic Party nominee for president." Though in the 2004 election, George W. Bush had enjoyed a lopsided 62 percent of the "born again" Christian vote as opposed to the 38 percent who voted for John Kerry, by 2008 a mere 29 percent of born again voters were committed to Republican candidates. Some 28 percent were unsure of who they would vote for, while more than 40 percent had already chosen to vote for a Democrat.[2] Scandals, loss of leadership, and the declining fortunes of the Bush administration were prying evangelical voters from their traditional moorings just when candidate Barack Obama was proclaiming a new brand of faith-based politics.

Adding to the dissolving influence of the Religious Right were the religious preferences of a rising new generation whom demographers reported would be voting in record numbers. Polls indicated that the majority of Americans ages seventeen to twenty-nine intended to vote for a Democrat in 2008 and that Barack Obama was their leading choice.[3] Moreover, it was not just his politics but his unorthodox spirituality that won them. Religiously, the majority of America's young are postmodern, which means they do faith like jazz: informal, eclectic, and often without theme. They have largely rejected organized religion in favor of a religious pastiche that works for them. They think nothing of hammering together a personal faith from widely differing religious traditions, and many acquire their theology the same way they catch colds: through casual contact with strangers. Thus, when Obama speaks of questioning certain tenets of his Christian faith or the importance of doubt in religion or his respect for non-Christian religions, the majority of the young instantly relate and welcome his nontraditional faith as a basis for his—and their— left-leaning politics.

> When Obama speaks of questioning certain tenets of his Christian faith, the young instantly relate and welcome his nontraditional faith as a basis for his—and their— left-leaning politics.

These three historic shifts—the

loss of the Religious Right's national leadership, the drift of born again voters toward the Democratic Party, and the religiously liberal, pro-Obama lean of young voters—changed the role of religion in the 2008 election. For a Religious Left just reclaiming its political voice, the marketplace of religious ideas in American politics was more open than at any time in a generation. It was a reality not lost on Barack Obama.

Also not lost on Obama are the possibilities of his astonishing popularity, which propels both his politics and his religious vision into the national psyche. He is regarded in American culture very much as Mark Nesbitt suggested on that afternoon in Boston before the now-storied convention speech: "like a rock star." He draws some of the largest and most enthusiastic crowds in American political history, he is backed by global celebrities like Tom Cruise and Oprah Winfrey, and he is considered the Midas touch for any political candidate he endorses. "We originally scheduled the Rolling Stones for this party," New Hampshire governor John Lynch joked at a rally. "But then we cancelled them when we realized that Senator Obama would sell more tickets." His many achievements become the building blocks of his legend. Oddly, one campaign book even reminds readers that Obama has won more Grammy Awards (two, for the recordings of his books *Dreams from My Father* and *The Audacity of Hope*) than Jimi Hendrix and Bob Marley combined (zero).[4]

There are, too, those connections that the faithful take as signposts of destiny. Obama filed his papers with the Federal Election

Commission in hopes of becoming the nation's first black president, one day after what would have been Martin Luther King Jr.'s, seventy-eighth birthday. Elected to the U.S. Senate, Obama was assigned the same desk that Robert F. Kennedy used, the culmination of a political journey begun forty years to the day after Kennedy was sworn in on January 4, 1965.

A sense of destiny is similarly suggested by the tale of his exotic background and the soul-searching it inspired. He has told this story in his two best-selling books, *Dreams from My Father* and *The Audacity of Hope*, both confirmation that Obama is among that rare breed of politicians who can write with skill and inspiration. His saga contains all the wrenching, ancient themes of human history and literature: the longing for place, the yearning for a father, the hope for a destiny. Like his politics, his life story is one that the public seems to embrace, and largely for its universal themes. In an unfathered, untethered generation, Obama often seems the Everyman in a heroic tale of spiritual seeking. Americans, as a people born of a religious vision, find in Obama at least a fellow traveler and at most a man at the vanguard of a new era of American spirituality.

There is also the appeal of his unusual openness, equally a function of his faith. In his books as in his speeches, he does not spare the details of drinking, drugs, sex, and dysfunction. He is a man comfortable with confession. This makes him a refreshing change from most American politicians. Asked by talk show host Jay Leno if he had inhaled when he smoked marijuana, Obama answered simply, "That was the point." His reply was typical of the transparent Obama charm and unself-conscious spirituality that many Americans have come to find so endearing.

> *Asked by talk show host Jay Leno if he had inhaled when he smoked marijuana, Obama answered simply, "That was the point."*

It is just such endearment that is winning adherents across the political spectrum. Obama himself tells of Republicans leaning in to him and saying in hushed voice, "I'm going to vote for you." He relates with mock puzzlement that his reply is often, "I'm glad." And then after a moment, "But why are we whispering?" Though his politics are decidedly liberal—his rating by the National Abortion Rights Action League is consistently 100 percent, his rating by the American Civil Liberties Union hovers around 80 percent, but his rating by the American Conservative Union is always in the single digits—he is drawing disaffected Republicans in surprising numbers.

These, then, are the dynamics that promise to train the magnetic pull of Obama's spirituality on American culture for years to come. He is unapologetically Christian and unapologetically liberal, and he believes that faith ought to inform his politics and that of the nation as a whole. Also important, he is handsome in a media age, well reasoned, and articulate, and he is not going away. Should he lose the presidential race in 2008, he can run for office as often as he likes for the next twenty-four years and still be younger than John McCain is as these words are written. In short, he is going to be a political and religious force to be reckoned with in American society, and both his supporters and his detractors are well served by understanding why.

What follows in these pages is an attempt to understand the religious life of Barack Obama and the changes in American religious history that he has come to represent. There is no attempt here to press a political agenda, nor is there a desire to rage against the realities of his life. Sufficient the rage of current American politics. This book is instead written in the belief that if a man's faith is sincere, it is the most important thing about him, and that it is impossible to understand who he is and how he will lead without first understanding the religious vision that informs his life. Equally important, there are often such riches of beauty and wisdom to be gained from a life informed by faith that the contemplation of it becomes its own reward. This is the spirit in which this book has been written.

Still, Barack Obama is a political being, and there can be no shrinking from the political implications of his faith. That it should be done kindly and generously is the insistence of this book. That it must be done at all is an insistence of the current religious vacuum in American political life.

1

To Walk Between Worlds

BOBBY RUSH IS AN IMPRESSIVE MAN. BORN IN THE DEEP South town of Albany, Georgia, in 1946, he later moved with his family to Chicago, Illinois, and rose to become a United States congressman. Along the way, he served in the U.S. Army, earned a bachelor's degree and two master's degrees, became an ordained Baptist minister, and won such respect in his district on the South Side of Chicago that he is now in his eighth term in office.

He also has the courage of his convictions. He was a cofounder of the Black Panther Party in Illinois and spent years operating a medical clinic and a breakfast program for children. He was a pioneer in drawing attention to the agonies of sickle cell anemia in the black community. Not surprising given his track record, on July 15, 2004, Congressman Rush became only the second sitting

U.S. congressman to be arrested—not for corruption or payola scams but for protesting human rights violations at the Sudanese Embassy in Washington, D.C.

Truly, Bobby Rush is an impressive man. So, why, in 1999, did thirty-eight-year-old Barack Obama, who had served in the Illinois senate only three years, decide to challenge Bobby Rush for his congressional seat? It could not have been the numbers. Rush's name recognition was more than 90 percent, while Obama's was barely 11. It also could not have been any political differences. Everyone knew that the two men held nearly the same views. It was one of the reasons that Rush often expressed hurt over Obama's challenge.

> *We must remember that if Obama ascends to the presidency in 2009, he will be the first American president to do so having not been raised in a Christian home.*

Whatever moved Obama to run against Rush, it was not a pleasant experience for the younger man. From the outset, Rush's approval rating was more than 70 percent. Then, not long into the campaign, Rush's son, Huey Rich, was tragically shot on his way home from a grocery store. The young man hung between life and death for four days. Though it was distasteful at the time for anyone to mention a political benefit to the tragedy, the outpouring of sympathy did seem to galvanize support for Rush, particularly among undecided voters. Soon billboards arose in the district, proclaiming, "I'm sticking with Bobby."

It never got better for Obama. Even President Clinton entered the fray and supported Rush, breaking his own policy of not endorsing candidates in primaries. Rush won with twice the vote Obama received—approximately 60 percent to 30 percent—and Obama was forced to admit that "[I got] my rear end handed to me."

There had been hurt and bitterness—the bad blood that fierce political battles can leave between men. Years went by, though, and with distance came a mellowing. The same Rush who had once described Obama as a man "blinded by ambition" came, in time, to a different view. After Obama entered the U.S. Senate, Rush said, "I think that Obama—his election to the Senate—was divinely ordered. I'm a preacher and pastor. I know that was God's plan. Obama has certain qualities. I think he is being used for some purpose."[1]

Rush is not alone in this. Increasingly, words such as *called*, *chosen*, and *anointed* are being used of Obama. Though these terms have long belonged to the native language of the Religious Right, they are now becoming the comfortable expressions of an awakened Religious Left, of a faith-based Progressive movement. Moreover, they are framing the image of Barack Obama in the minds of millions of Americans.

Perhaps this should be expected. Perhaps this is nothing more than a by-product of the uniquely American need to paint politics and politicians in messianic terms. Perhaps this is what comes, in part, from a people believing themselves a chosen nation.

Yet what is unique about the use of such terms as applied to Barack Obama is how foreign they are to the religious worldview of his early life. We must remember that if he ascends to the presidency in 2009, he will be the first American president to do so having not been raised in a Christian home. Instead, he spent his early years under the influence of atheism, folk Islam, and a humanist's understanding of the world that sees religion merely as a man-made thing, as a product of psychology. It is this departure from tradition in Obama's early years that makes both his political journey and his religious journey so unusual and of such symbolic meaning in American public life.

The story of the religious influences that have shaped Barack Obama is best begun with the novel faith of his grandmother, Madelyn Payne. She was born in 1922 to strict Methodist parents in the oil boom town of Augusta, Kansas. Though modern Methodists are known more for their eagerness to accommodate the sensitivities of secular society—removing offensive "gender bias" from their hymns, for example—the Midwest Methodists of the 1920s and 1930s exacted a higher price for righteousness. There was no drinking, card playing, or dancing in the Payne household. In church on Sundays, the family heard often of how small the army of the saved truly is compared to the vast numbers of those in the world who are going to hell. There were, too, the petty tyrannies that often attend religion in a flawed world: people shunned one another, lived lives at odds with the gospel they claimed to hold dear, and failed to distinguish themselves in any meaningful way from the world around them.

These hypocrisies were not lost on Madelyn Payne. She would tell her grandson often of the "sanctimonious preachers" she had known and of the respectable church ladies with absurd hats who whispered hurtful secrets and treated those they deemed beneath them with cruelty. What folly, she would recall with disgust, that a people would be taught to ignore all the geologic evidence and believe that the earth and the heavens had been created in seven days. What injustice, she would insist, that men who sat on church boards should utter "racial epithets" and cheat the men who worked for them. Barack regularly heard such bitter sentiments in his grandparents' home, sentiments that profoundly shaped his early religious worldview.

Madelyn was frequently described by neighbors as "different," a gentle word for her eccentricities, and few were likely surprised when she met, and then secretly married, Stanley Dunham, a furniture salesman from nearby El Dorado. If the marriage was not exactly the attraction of opposites, it was at least the blending of incongruities. He was notoriously loud, crashing, and gregarious; friends said he could "charm the legs off of a couch." She was bookish and sensitive. He was a Baptist from a blue-collar world. She was a Methodist whose parents were solidly middle class. Though in their generation these seemingly slight differences were enough to separate couples of less determination, Stanley and Madelyn fell in love and later married on the night of a junior/senior prom just weeks before her high school graduation in 1940. For reasons that remain unclear, her parents were not told of the union until her diploma was well in hand. They did not receive the news well, though this seemed to make little difference to the headstrong and increasingly rebellious Madelyn.

With the onset of World War II, Stanley enlisted in the army and ended up slogging through Europe with General George Patton's tank corps without ever seeing real combat. Madelyn worked as a riveter at the Boeing Company's B-29 plant in Wichita. In late November 1942, their daughter, Ann Dunham, was born.

Stanley Dunham has been described as a kind of Willy Loman,

the tragic, broken character in Arthur Miller's *Death of a Salesman*. There are similarities. Returning from war and grasping the promise of the GI Bill, Stanley moved his young family to California, where he enrolled at the University of California–Berkeley. Obama would later recount kindly of his grandfather that "the classroom couldn't contain his ambitions, his restlessness, and so the family moved on."[2] It was the pattern of a lifetime. There was first a return to Kansas and then years of one small Texas town after another, one dusty furniture store leading to the promise of bigger rewards at still another store farther up the road.

Finally, in 1955, just as Ann finished the seventh grade, the family moved to Seattle, where Stanley acquired a job as a salesman for Standard-Grunbaum Furniture, a recognized feature of the downtown area at the corner of Second and Pine. For most of their five years in Seattle, the family lived on Mercer Island, "a South America-shaped stretch of Douglas firs and cedars," which lay across from the city in Lake Washington.[3] While Stanley sold living room suites and Madelyn worked for a bank, young Ann began drinking from the troubled currents of the counterculture just then beginning to sweep through American society.

The high school that Ann attended was far from the stereotypical 1950s image. In the very year that she began classes at Mercer High, John Stenhouse, chairman of the school's board, admitted before the House Un-American Activities Subcommittee that he was a member of the Communist Party. Already at Mercer, there were recurring parental firestorms over the curriculum, long before such conflicts became commonplace throughout the nation. Most complaints centered on the ideas of Val Foubert and Jim Wichterman, two instructors who were perceived as so radical for the time that students called the passageway between their classrooms "Anarchy Hall." Together the two men had determined, without apology, to incite their students to both question and challenge all authority.

Foubert, who taught English, assigned books such as *Atlas Shrugged, The Organization Man, The Hidden Persuaders, 1984,* and the most strident of H. L. Mencken's cultural commentaries—none of which are extreme by today's standard but which were certainly out of the mainstream in 1950s America. Wichterman, who taught philosophy, assigned Sartre, Kierkegaard, and Karl Marx's *The Communist Manifesto,* and did not hesitate to question the existence of God. Parental upheavals ensued, which Foubert and Wichterman dubbed "Mother Marches." "The kids started questioning things that their folks thought shouldn't be questioned—religion, politics, parental authority," John Hunt, a student at the time, remembered, "and a lot of parents didn't like that and tried to get them [Wichterman and Foubert] fired."[4]

None of this upheaval was of much concern to Stanley and Madelyn Dunham, though. Having long before shed the quaint faith and suffocating values of rural Kansas, Ann's parents were comfortable with the innovations in the Mercer High School curriculum. They had even begun attending East Shore Unitarian Church in nearby Bellevue—often referred to in Seattle as "the little Red church on the hill"—for its liberal theology and politics. Barack would later describe this as the family's "only skirmish into organized religion" and explain that Stanley "liked the idea that Unitarians drew on the scriptures of all the great religions," excitedly proclaiming, "It's like you get five religions in one!" "For

Christ's sake," Madelyn would shoot back, according to Barack, "It's not supposed to be like buying breakfast cereal!"[5]

Though what has come to be known as the Unitarian Affirmation of Faith is, in fact, an overly simplistic reworking of the ideas of James Freeman Clarke, it does serve to hint at what the Dunhams accepted as true: "the fatherhood of God, the brotherhood of man, the leadership of Jesus, salvation by character, and the progress of mankind onward and upward forever." That Stanley and Madelyn believed in a God of some description is confirmed by Barack. However, they were likely skeptics—Barack says that Madelyn espoused a "flinty rationalism"—regarding the divinity of Jesus, whom they would have accepted as one good moral teacher among many but certainly not a god. That man is perfectible, that men ought to live as brothers, and that society would climb ever upward if they did are all truths that were agreed upon in the Dunham home, though Ann would in time accept these possibilities only on the most secular terms.

In truth, Ann Dunham was already on a journey beyond the freethinking of her parents, beyond her friends at Mercer High School, and yet in keeping with the philosophical trends of her times. She had absorbed the broad spirituality and social vision of the East Shore Unitarian Church. She had also been paying attention in the classrooms of Foubert and Wichterman. Having begun with her parents' religious skepticism, Ann went even further and declared herself an atheist.

During after-school gab sessions in the coffee shops of Seattle, her friends began to realize how fully Ann had thought through her beliefs. "She touted herself as an atheist, and it was something she'd read about and could argue," remembers Maxine Box, who was Dunham's best friend in high school. "She was always challenging and arguing and comparing. She was already thinking about things that the rest of us hadn't." Another classmate, Jill Burton-Dascher, recalls that Ann "was intellectually way more mature than we were and a little bit ahead of her time, in an off-center way." "If you were concerned about something going wrong in the world," Chip Wall, a friend, explains, "[Ann] would know about it first." She was, he says, "a fellow traveler. . . . We were liberals before we knew what liberals were."[6]

As the decade of the 1960s dawned and Ann approached the end of her high school career, friends expected she might chart a bold course: college at a European university perhaps, or studies back east among the nation's Ivy League. They soon heard that Stanley had found a new job—yet another furniture store with yet bolder promises of success—this time in Hawaii. Though some remember that Ann did not want to go, it was not long before letters began arriving from Honolulu, describing how she had enrolled in the University of Hawaii for the fall term of 1960.

Only the year before, Hawaii had achieved statehood. This was likely part of the attraction for Stanley. His adventurous, ever-unsatisfied soul yearned for what appeared to be a new frontier. A fresh start in a new state, far from the American mainland, seemed ideal. He was entering his forties—the onset of midlife crisis for most men—his only daughter had just finished high school, and the darkness of the 1960s had yet to descend. Life was full of promise, though for Stanley this would mean going where that promise lived: a new place, a new role, a new crowd to charm.

> *Stanley could not have known that his life would be both graced and anguished by the comings and goings of his daughter and the little biracial boy she would bring into the world.*

He could not have known that it would be the last move of his life or that he would eventually pass his days in a small Honolulu apartment, if not embittered then at least disillusioned by his few achievements. He could not have known that in the meantime, his wife would rise to become the first female vice president of the Bank of Hawaii and would do so without a college degree, an astonishing achievement for a woman in that era. And he could not have known that his life would be both graced and anguished by the comings and goings of his daughter and the little biracial boy she would bring into the world.

Ann Dunham met Barack Obama Sr. while she was a freshman and he a graduate student at the University of Hawaii. He must have appeared exotic to her, with his rich, full voice; his Kenyan accent; his chiseled features; and his studied worldliness. He had come to Hawaii on the wings of extreme good fortune: his government had sent him abroad to study on a scholarship created for the rising leaders of Jomo Kenyatta's Kenya. Though he now spent weekends with Ann, listening to jazz, drinking beer, and debating politics and world affairs with their friends, he had only a few years before lived a Kenyan village life, herding goats and submitting to the rituals of a village witch doctor. Now, in the West, he had rejected the Muslim faith of his youth just as he rejected the babblings of all witch doctors. Religion is superstition, he insisted. It falls to man to fashion his own fate and the fate of his nation. This was what he intended to do when he finished school and returned to Kenya.

Things moved quickly for Ann and her new love. Sometime late in the fall of 1960, she conceived a child. Several months into 1961, she and Barack married, and six months later, friends in Seattle were receiving letters announcing the birth of their son, Barack Hussein Obama, born August 4, 1961.

What followed immediately after is now well-known. Barack Obama Sr. continued to live in Hawaii only a short time after the birth of the son who bore his name. An opportunity to earn his doctorate at Harvard proved too enticing, and he left, to return only once more before his death in 1982 of alcohol, bitterness, and a car crash. The pictures of young Barack make it hard to imagine any father walking away from such a child. In time, Ann and Barack would learn that Barack Sr. had been married in a Kenyan village ceremony long before he met Ann and already had other children. She would file for divorce in 1964.

There are many things to admire about Ann and how she raised her son, and certainly among them is the way she kept the positive memory of Barack Obama Sr. alive in her son's heart. Though a less-generous soul might speak only ill of such a man, Ann regularly rehearsed his virtues to young Barack. The boy knew nearly from birth that his father had grown up poor in a poor country on a poor continent, and that only through hard work and toughness had he risen to esteem. "Your brains, your character, you got from him," she assured him, and so worked to keep a deforming bitterness from settling into her son's spirit.

The years after Barack Sr.'s departure, and while the family was still in Hawaii, were nearly idyllic for young Barack. There were frequent trips with Grandfather Stanley to the Ali'i Park, joyous days at the beach, and adventures such as deep-sea fishing off Kailua Bay that seared themselves happily into his memory. A photograph survives from this time of Barack swinging a baseball bat nearly as long as he is. It is an image of a child who is loved and content, a picture taken by a member of the family who clearly delights in those spindly legs, that broad smile, that beautifully shaped head. Madelyn, whom young Barack called "Toot"—short for the Hawaiian word for grandmother, *Tutu*—read to her grandson by the hour, eager to pass along the literary joys she had known as a child through the Great Books her family ordered by mail on the plains of Kansas. These were happy times. The haunting of race, rootlessness, and an absent father are for later years.

Creeping into Barack's remembrance of these years is a man named Lolo Soetoro, a friend and a fellow student of his mother's at the University of Hawaii. He soon after became Barack's wrestling partner and Stanley's loyal opponent in chess. Within two years, he was more, and Ann told her son that Lolo had proposed marriage, that she had accepted, and that it meant they would move to the other side of the world, to a place called Indonesia.

It says much about Ann Dunham Soetoro that she would uproot her son from the glories of Hawaii and move him in the mid-1960s to one of the most troubled places on earth. Indonesia had been led for decades by its revolutionary founder, Sukarno, a man more adept at words than administration. He had attempted to build his country on five ideals he called the Five Fundamental Principles: nationalism, internationalism, democracy, social prosperity, and belief in God. These were intended to be the essence of the Indonesian spirit. However, Sukarno's era in Indonesia is testament that words alone do not make a nation. By the 1960s, Sukarno's ineptitude had led to widespread suffering. As historian Paul Johnson has written: "Food rotted in the countryside. The towns starved. Foreign investment vanished."[7] Meanwhile, Sukarno's personal behavior became an international scandal. He acquired wives and mistresses freely, and his foreign jaunts were famous for his sexual foraging. During a visit to Indonesia in 1960, Soviet premier Nikita Khrushchev was shocked to see Sukarno chatting happily and openly with a completely naked woman.[8]

To cover the disasters of his leadership, Sukarno secretly gave the nod to a coup by the Communist Party in 1965. Sukarno's generals and handpicked officials were murdered, their daughters raped, the bodies of their wives and children thrown into the Lubang Buaja, the Crocodile Hole. The coup failed, however, and a General Suharto, the strategic reserve commander, took over. In a bloody backlash against the communists, hundreds of thousands were butchered, perhaps as many as a million. These horrors slowed to an end in 1966, only a year before Ann began to raise her six-year-old son in Jakarta.

The years that young Barack's family lived in Indonesia will likely remain among the most controversial of his life. The facts are simple enough, though. The family initially lived in a small, flat-roofed bungalow at 16 Haji Ramli Street. Barack, who was known as Barry in these years, ran the dirt streets around his house, wearing a sarong, the traditional wraparound skirt worn by men, and played soccer by the hour with the neighborhood children. Because Lolo, his stepfather, was a Muslim, young Barry was listed as Muslim in official documents. Occasionally, he accompanied Lolo to a nearby mosque on Fridays and prayed at his side for the blessings of Allah.

> Barack accompanied Lolo to a nearby mosque on Fridays and prayed at his side for the blessings of Allah.

In 1968, Barry began first grade at St. Francis Assisi Foundation School, which was a few blocks from his home. As each school day began, he would cross himself, pray the Hail Mary, the Our Father, and whatever else the attending nuns required. The atheist Ann and the Muslim Lolo endured this Catholic influence because the education at the school was among the best available. Two years later, after Lolo landed a job with an oil company and moved the family to a better neighborhood, Barack entered a public school now called Model Primary School Menteng 1. Here again, Barack was listed as a Muslim, which meant that he studied the doctrines of Islam during the required two hours a week of religious instruction.

His life was a religious swirl. He lived in a largely Muslim country. He prayed at the feet of a Catholic Jesus. He attended a mosque with his stepfather and learned Islam in his public school. At home, his mother taught him her atheistic optimism. She was, wrote Obama years later, "a lonely witness for secular humanism, a soldier for New Deal, Peace Corps, position-paper liberalism."⁹

Lolo's faith was more complex. Though he called himself a Muslim and urged Islam on Ann and Barack as a means to connect to the community, he was not very religious. This is surprising to many contemporary Westerners who think of Islam only in terms of the strident, fundamentalist strain that is causing so much heartache in the world today. Indonesia in the late 1960s and early 1970s was often violent for political reasons, but seldom for the sake of religion. The Islam of Indonesia in those days easily blended with Hinduism, Buddhism, and even animism, to produce a broad, eclectic spirituality. The daily experience of this blend is best described as folk Islam, a superstitious and occult fringe faith comprised largely of rituals to drive away evil: incantations against the evil eye, charms to ward off spirits, symbols to assure blessing, and ancient understanding of spiritual power and its uses.

Lolo lived on the folk edge of Islam, teaching young Barack superstitions and rituals popular on the streets of Jakarta. He believed, for example, that a man took on the powers of whatever he ate, a cherished pagan notion through the centuries. He often brought tiger meat home in hopes of making his stepson a fiercer, more powerful man. Yet the doctrines of orthodox Islam held little sway with Lolo. For example, he employed a young male cook who liked to dress up as a woman on weekends, something a more faithful Muslim would never have allowed in his home. Indeed, the young man's life would have been in peril among fundamentalists. Lolo also loved women, drink, and Western music. Barack would later recall his stepfather's passion for Johnny Walker Black and

Andy Williams records. "Moon River" was nearly the soundtrack of his Indonesian memories.

Obama has written that his mother taught him to view religion as "a phenomenon to be treated with a suitable respect, but with a suitable detachment as well."[10] It is just this detachment that may have proven the greatest emotional lesson of his years in Indonesia. He was to live in a Muslim country but be taught by his stepfather's example to ignore the most fundamental teachings of Islam. He was to attend a Roman Catholic school, but regard Christianity as no more than superstition. And he was to love a mother who viewed all religion as nothing more than a man-made tool for contending with the mysteries of life. Only through a steely shielding of the heart, only through a determined detachment, could a child of Barack's age be exposed to so much incongruous religious influence and emerge undamaged. Perhaps, though, the damage was in the detachment itself.

> His stepfather lived on the folk edge of Islam, teaching young Barack superstitions and rituals popular on the streets of Jakarta.

The question that will surface again and again about Obama's years in Indonesia is this: Was Barack Obama a Muslim? If he was a true Muslim, then his conversion to Christianity in his later years would make him *murtadd* in the eyes of Muslims: an apostate. Orthodox Islam would insist that such a man be rejected by his community and, in some jurisdictions, marked for death.

This extremism regarding apostates is not buried in an earlier age of Islam but is still very much alive and has actually intensified in recent decades. The revered and controversial Pakistani scholar Sayyid Abul Ala Maududi, for example, argued fiercely for the execution of

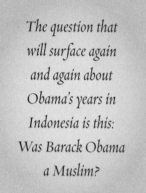

The question that will surface again and again about Obama's years in Indonesia is this: Was Barack Obama a Muslim?

apostates, and his thinking is typical of the reasoning that might be applied to Barack Obama's story:

The heart of the matter is that children born of Muslim lineage will be considered Muslims and according to Islamic law the door of apostasy will never be opened to them. If anyone of them renounces Islam, he will be as deserving of execution as the person who has renounced *kufr* [infidelity to Islam] to become a Muslim and again has chosen the way of *kufr*. All the jurists of Islam agree with this decision. On this topic absolutely no difference exists among the experts of *shari'ah*.[11]

The question of whether Obama fits this description is complicated somewhat by the way a man becomes a Muslim. In Islam, a man submits to Allah and enters the community of faith by reciting the creed *There is no God but Allah, and Muhammad is his Prophet.* These are the words a Muslim speaks over his newborn child and hopes to have upon his own lips at his death. They are the keys to faith, the pathway of conversion.

Did young Barack say these words in honor of Islam? Yes,

certainly, both at his stepfather's side in the Jakarta mosque on Fridays and in the Islamic religious instruction he received several hours a week in school. Does this make him a Muslim in his childhood and therefore a *murtadd* now? Neither the Koran nor the *Hadith*, the systematic compilation of Muslim teaching, addresses this issue. The question seems to vary from jurisdiction to jurisdiction, but the majority opinion among Islamic teachers, despite Maududi's insistence to the contrary, is that a child must have reached puberty before his confession of faith amounts to a full conversion. Barack was years from puberty in his last months in Indonesia, so he is not to be considered a full convert to Islam, and therefore he is not an apostate now.

It is an interesting question, and one that will likely surface often. If Barack Obama should ascend to the presidency and offend Islamic mullahs by his policies, there could conceivably be a *fatwa* [religious decree] issued against him from some renegade jurisdiction on the basis that he is an apostate. It would be untrue, of course, in light of the consensus of Islamic teaching. Still, some enraged mullah might take note that Obama's biological father was an apostate from Islam. This could be held alongside his own childhood confession of faith as sufficient evidence to rule him a *murtadd* and deserving of death. It would all be a lie, of course, and

> *These early morning sessions and the mental rigors they required may well have been the spark of the intellectual fires that gave him, ultimately, an exceptional mind.*

nothing more than a manufactured excuse for murder. Nevertheless, it would be the first time in American history that such a charge could be engineered against a sitting president.

Though religion permeated Barry's years in Indonesia, what may have had an even greater impact on the course of his life were his mother's efforts to give him a superior education. This came in the wake of a decline in Ann and Lolo's relationship and her realization that she did not want to lose Barack to Indonesia. She long had preached the virtues of cultural sensitivity, of never becoming a boorish outsider to the indigenous people. Now, she began to fear that the tentacles of this strange land were wrapped too tightly around her son. No, she would not lose him to the East. He would be an American, she determined, and education was the best way to make this so.

From the time they arrived in Jakarta, she had supplemented his local schooling with a correspondence course from the States. Determined to seal her son to the West, Ann redoubled her efforts. Each morning, she awakened her son at 4:00 a.m., fed and dressed him, and began drilling him in English for three hours before he traipsed off to school. It was not a pleasant experience. Barry resisted, claimed illness, and generally fought his mother at every step. In time, the lessons took hold, and Barry began to show a facility for language and learning that surprised even Ann. Though it could not have seemed the case at the time, these early morning sessions and the mental rigors they required may well have been the spark of the intellectual fires that gave him, ultimately, an exceptional mind.

These efforts were evidence that Ann had turned her attention to America. The progression that followed is unclear, perhaps by design. Obama's little sister, Maya, was born, and not long afterward Ann made plans for Barack to return to the States. Ann and Maya initially remained in Indonesia and then in a matter of months returned to America. There followed a divorce. The three—Ann, Barack, and Maya—would see Lolo only once more in their lives, when he traveled to Los Angeles ten years later for treatment of the liver ailment that ultimately killed him at the age of fifty-one.

Upon his return to Honolulu in 1971, Barack was enrolled in the esteemed Punahou School. It was a turning point in his young life, one that determined much that would follow. Until then, other than the intelligence his mother recognized in him, there seemed to be little exceptional about his life. He lived with middle-class grandparents and followed his quixotic mother as she chased her loves and her dreams. He was a bright ten year old, but nothing as yet indicated the promise of his life: nothing concretely presaged the ascent to come. Punahou was the beginning of distinction.

He gained admission through the good graces of his grand-father's boss, an alumnus of the school. After interviews and testing, Barack was admitted and thus became part of a tradition that dated to 1841, when Punahou was founded to educate the children of Hawaii's Congregational missionaries. In the more than a century and a half since, it had become "an incubator for the island elites."[12] Barack was a student there for a vital seven years of his life. Academically and athletically, he thrived. He maintained a solid B average, threw himself into his love of basketball, and even wrote for the school's literary magazine.

Yet in these years he also began the agonizing search for belonging as a man of mixed race. Who was he really? What tribe could he claim as his own? Mixed in with his natural adolescent search for both freedom and definition was a more subterranean yearning to belong to a like people, to have a place among a nation of like kind. Hawaii did not make this easy. It offered too much, seemed to affirm too many options. There was no prescribed path, no single style or type that stood out. In hotel rooms, along with the Gideon Bible, guests were often surprised to find both the Book of Mormon and the Teachings of the Buddha. Every ethnic and religious option was represented on the streets of Honolulu. Even at Punahou, the clocks in the library showed the times in Third World nations, an attempt by the administration to reinforce its message of multiculturalism. None of this made it easy for Barack to single out his unique place in the world.

During his years at Punahou, he tried on personas as another man might try on clothes. Was he the angry radical brother or the educated, upwardly mobile black? Was he intent upon destroying the system or rising within it? Should he drift in bitterness into drugs and parties—and gripe sessions where he poured out his excuses for failure—or should he nurse an "I'll show them," angry drive and take on the world? Was it denying his blackness to date a white girl or running from his white world to socialize only with blacks? More vitally, was he fully any one thing in

> *During Obama's years at Punahou, he tried on personas as another man might try on clothes. Was he the angry radical brother or the educated, upwardly mobile black?*

the world? White? Black? American? He wasn't sure. He read Baldwin, Ellison, Hughes, Wright, and Dubois, but found no map for the country he sought. All of them ended, he concluded, "exhausted, bitter men, the devil at their heels."[13]

Graduating from Punahou in 1979, he attended Occidental University in Los Angeles for two years but found himself sinking into the aimlessness of some of his friends. He knew he had to pull himself out of the bog. He decided to transfer to Columbia University in New York, and there followed what he later described as a "fundamental rupture in my life." He had not come to a grand plan and certainly had no political ambitions. Yet he did decide that he wanted to, as he put it, "make my mark," that he yearned to be noticed, to do something important—perhaps even to live an exceptional life.[14] He became more serious about his future but was still aware that he had "no guide that might show [him] how to join this troubled world." When he slipped into the back pew of New York's Abyssinian Baptist Church one Sunday and felt the sweet sorrow in an ancient song, he was void of the faith that gave the song wings. He belonged there and didn't, much as it was for him in the world. He was, as his sister, Maya, would later say, walking "between worlds."[15]

The truth is he was lonely. By the time he finished college with a degree in political science in 1983, he was living half a world away from his only family. His father, whom he had not seen in more than a decade, had recently died. It is possible that having learned detachment from his anthropologist mother, he had made detachment a lifestyle. He was in a self-imposed prison, one created by both his need and his curse to look upon the world as though he were not a part of it. He became a rootless wanderer and was haunted by "the mixed blood, the divided soul, the ghostly image of the tragic mulatto trapped between two worlds."[16]

This was his state when he landed in Chicago in 1985. He had recently tasted work in the New York corporate world and found it thin. Arriving in a city he barely knew, he went to work for a social improvement organization called Developing Communities Project. His Herculean task was to mobilize people on Chicago's South Side to make positive change in their community. His world now became the roiling, largely black, deeply frustrated, poverty-ridden yet often joyful streets of the neighborhoods that gave the world both the music of Muddy Waters and the fiction of Upton Sinclair. Obama gave himself to any cause important to the people—from asbestos to crime, from church unity to prostitution—as a means of building consensus and thus political power. He spent many of his days interviewing people about their needs and complaints. He called meetings, cajoled, endured repeated humiliation, and enjoyed minor victories. He was ambitious and came to see the connection between crisis and power. As he wrote later in *Dreams from My Father*, "Issues, action, power, self-interest. I liked these concepts. They bespoke a certain hardheadedness, a worldly lack of sentiment; politics, not religion."[17]

Yet religion became his crisis, personally and professionally. He admitted to coworkers that he was "not very religious" and was told that this only put a barrier between himself and the people. In the community, people wanted to know where he got his faith before they wanted to hear his ideas for social improvement. But he had no faith, not in the religious sense. His work with pastors hadn't helped that cause. Though he found some clergymen who were willing to roll up their sleeves and work to heal the community, many pastors he met were either politicians with clerical collars or men who were too tradition-bound to be of any use—or to offer any refreshment to his parched soul.

He was also pressing against the limits of his mother's worldview, and it was a disturbing experience.

> I had no community or shared traditions in which to ground my most deeply held beliefs. The Christians with whom I worked recognized themselves in me; they saw that I knew their Book and shared their values and sang their songs. But they sensed that a part of me remained removed, *detached*, an observer among them. I came to realize that without a vessel for my beliefs, without an unequivocal commitment to a particular community of faith, I would be consigned at some level to always remain apart, free in the way that my mother was free, but also alone in the same ways she was ultimately alone.[18]

Ann had loved him, imparted to him a sense of the power of his gifts, and cheered him on as he rose in the world. Much of what he became was due to her devotion. Yet she could not give him what she did not have. As a woman who had rejected faith and looked upon human society much as a scientist looks at cells through a microscope, she paid the price for her detachment by ultimately having no belonging, no tribe, no people to claim for her own. Though she could be a warm and broadly spiritual person, she was isolated by the detachment she prized. Her legacy might have been his own had he not come to realize the horrible price of her beliefs.

It was as these thoughts troubled his mind that Barack Obama landed in a pew at the 8:00 a.m. Sunday service of Trinity United Church of Christ. He had met some weeks before with the pastor, Jeremiah Wright, though the topic of the discussion had been the community and how Trinity was often perceived by other churches. Obama had a dual agenda. He listened respectfully as Wright talked, but he was also scanning the spirit of the man and testing the waters in light of a change he was considering. The meeting ended, Obama grabbed some material about the church at the front office as he left, and then he let weeks go by.

He was wrestling—with his conscience, his cynicism, his intellectual approach to faith. Asked if he would join a friend at church, he demurred.

> And I would shrug and play the question off, unable to confess that I could no longer distinguish between faith and mere folly, between faith and simple endurance; that while I believed in the sincerity I heard in their voices, I remained a reluctant skeptic, doubtful of my own motives, wary of expedient conversion, having too many quarrels with God to accept a salvation too easily won.[19]

Nevertheless, questions raging and doubts unresolved, he came. As he sat in that Trinity pew early that Sunday morning, he settled into the comforting mercies of the African-American church. He knew that this church, like most of its kind, had long ministered to the community as it did to the man, that individual salvation and collective salvation were both noble goals of the black gospel. This idea pleased him. He also felt peace at the notion that in the black church "the lines between sinner and saved were more fluid," that "you needed to embrace Christ precisely because you had sins to wash away" and not because you walked in the door perfect as a glowing gift for God.[20] This he needed to know as he sat there, a man of doubt and conflict.

The sermon that day was on a topic that would live in his soul and in his politics. It was called "The Audacity of Hope." In the skilled rhetorical hands of Jeremiah Wright, the lesson mounted into a grand symphony of uniquely African-American preaching. Searing biblical content was overlaid against social commentary and all brought to bear on the sufferings and promised victories of each individual life in the congregation. Somehow, beginning with the slender hopes of Hannah, the mother of the prophet Samuel, Rev. Wright managed to reflect on the injustices of Sharpsville and Hiroshima, the follies of state and federal government in America, and the callousness of the middle class. Despite the broad range of references, or perhaps because of them, a laser of hope penetrated Barack's soul. At sermon's end, he found himself in tears.

It was a beginning. The process that followed took months and could not be hurried. And when the turning came, it was not attended by angels and flashes of light. In the retelling it did not have the ring of the famous conversions of history, with their great moral transformations and dramatic encounters with God. Instead, it was a decision to enter a faith by joining a people of faith, to come home to a community and so come home to God. Indeed, as Obama has explained, "It came about as a choice and not an epiphany; the questions I had did not magically disappear. But kneeling beneath that cross on the South Side of Chicago, I felt God's spirit beckoning me. I submitted myself to His will and dedicated myself to discovering His truth."[21]

2

My House, Too

Presidential candidate Sam Brownback was feeling relieved. Appearing with Barack Obama at a 2006 World AIDS Day summit sponsored by Rick Warren's Saddleback Church, Brownback said he felt a bit more "comfortable" than he had the last time the two presidential candidates shared a stage. "We were both addressing the NAACP," he told the crowd of several thousand. "They were very polite to me. I think they kind of wondered, 'Who's this guy from Kansas?' And then Barack Obama follows, and they're going, 'Okay, now we've got Elvis.'"

Assuming that Warren's evangelical church would be home turf for a conservative Roman Catholic like himself, Brownback then turned to Obama and said, "Welcome to *my* house!" The audience exploded with laughter and applause. A few moments later, though,

Obama took the stage and said, "There is one thing I have to say, Sam. This is my house, too. This is God's house."[1]

Once again, Obama showed his skill at intercepting the political long pass. Brownback intended an appeal to his base. Obama wasn't having it. Refusing to yield an inch of the religious high ground, he made it clear to all that not only would he not be moved from his rightful place in the Christian fold, but he also would not allow newcomers to the crisis of AIDS, newcomers like Warren's evangelicals, to forget that Obama's political tribe began addressing that issue long ago. *Be a Christian with me, Sam,* he was saying, *but don't act like my older brother. This is my house, too.*

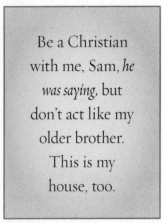

Be a Christian with me, Sam, *he was saying,* but don't act like my older brother. This is my house, too.

Though Obama was declaring his membership in the universal house of God, his more local house of faith is far removed from Rick Warren's Saddleback Church and the largely white enclaves of Lake Forest, California. Instead, Obama's spiritual house sits nearly half a continent away, in the heart of housing projects and steel mesh–wrapped businesses on Chicago's black and proud South Side.

A visitor to a Sunday morning service at Trinity United Church of Christ is first struck by the worshippers who walk the weary streets of their South Side neighborhood en route to their spiritual home. Mothers balance on high heels while wrestling handfuls of fussy children along broken sidewalks; fathers make a game of carrying sweetly dressed daughters on broad shoulders past the never-quiet traffic on West Ninety-fifth Street. Some have walked for miles, yet there is determination in each step born of a spiritual hunger and a universal yearning to assume a place among one's people.

Drawing near to the impressive yellow-beige building that houses Trinity Church, the visitor also senses the care and planning that pervades the life of this spiritual family. Kind but imposing security men are positioned strategically around the building, each dressed stylishly for church but with earbuds and walkie-talkies protruding. Some are armed, as has become the unfortunate need of many large churches around the nation. Stepping from the obviously loved and tenderly maintained grounds through the main doors, the visitor is greeted by older men and women who put the loving face on this carefully crafted system of hospitality.

If the visitor is late, he may well be asked to stand in lines defined by velvet ropes and fastened to brass stands, much as he might see at an upscale movie theater. The message is clear: *This is not just a church; this is a cultural phenomenon, a religious experience of historic importance for the people who attend.* Hundreds throng to enter, sometimes arriving in the still-dark hours of the morning just to get a seat. Don't be late.

Passing through the lobby, the visitor might easily miss the first symbols of the defining vision of this people. A picture of a black Jesus hangs behind an information desk, His arms extended around a black family radiating joy and contentment. There are, too, black faces in the biblical scenes depicted in the glorious stained glass of Trinity Church. These are silent testimony to the theological vision at the heart of this African-American family of faith.

While the crowd begins to fill up the nearly twenty-seven hundred seats of the contemporary-style sanctuary, the visitor cannot help but notice the clothing of the worshippers. There are, of course, the brilliant dresses, hats, and fashionable suits one expects of a black church in America. There is also more casual attire—jeans and leather jackets; stepping-out-at-night, low-cut dresses; and even work clothes worn by the city bus driver who did not have time to change. All are welcome. Yet in larger numbers than most black churches can boast, the worshippers at this church dress in the attire of Africa. Dashikis and flowing robes sing their colors in African hues, and huge turbans bound with exotic knots are worn by women who understand the power of the statement they make. One quickly realizes that this is not a fashion show: these are the uniforms of a worldview.

Ushers wearing white gloves seat all comers, while older women keep a mothering eye on the waiting crowd. "Sir, is that a recording device? Oh, your electronic Bible? Okay then, enjoy the service." "Ma'am, we don't allow cameras. May I ask you to put that away until you leave the grounds?" All is done with kindness and grace, yet with the underlying firmness of elders tending their clan.

Indeed, the whole system of gathering has obviously been crafted with an eye to serving the outsider while protecting church members from intrusion. This is, after all, a spiritual family of nearly ten thousand, where a U.S. senator and the most famous woman in America, Oprah Winfrey, sometimes attend. Members of the press are kindly tagged and assigned a handler. Attendees smile knowingly at an unshaven French camera crew in jeans and boots, now escorted by an elegant Nigerian woman in a brilliantly colored gown, explaining what may and may not be done. Reporters who stray off-limits may well be met by mountainous security men, some former members of the Chicago Bears, who gently suggest a return to bounds.

At the exact moment of the published starting time, a woman moves to the pulpit to make announcements. So striking is her manner that years after seeing her for the first time, Barack Obama remembered the "graying hair" and "no-nonsense demeanor." At her first word, the crowd immediately falls to silence. This is a disciplined congregation.

If the visitor does not allow himself to be bored by this ritual of information sharing common to all churches, he may come to understand something of the soul of this people from these few introductory moments. Careful attention over time will reveal that on a budget of nearly $10 million—respectable but not exceptional for a church of its size—Trinity sponsors more than seventy ministries and dozens of educational institutions around the world. There are alcohol and drug-addiction outreaches, ex-offender programs, hospices, counseling services, elder care, and many other social services of nearly every kind. The church has given more than a million dollars to the United Negro College Fund and has raised hundreds of thousands to support

> *On a budget of nearly $10 million—respectable but not exceptional for a church of its size—Trinity sponsors more than seventy ministries and dozens of educational institutions around the world.*

scholarships and schools, some as far away as Africa and the Middle East. There are academic programs, college preparatory services, and even college fairs. Consciously resisting a "silo mentality," in which wealth is stored but not used, Trinity clearly intends to invest wealth to change the culture of its people. It also clearly intends to break from the black church of tradition. Trinity sponsors a large outreach to gay and lesbian singles, an emphasis both unusual and controversial among African-American Christians.

Listening a bit more closely, the visitor may come to understand that this is not just a congregation of the downtrodden. There are in attendance multimillionaire businessmen, politicians, medical doctors, and hundreds of teachers and college professors, including at least a dozen from the prestigious University of Chicago. The church is sometimes criticized in its own community for being too "buppie": black, upwardly mobile, professional. This fact does not seem to bother the pastors. Several of them hold degrees from Ivy League schools, and no senior staffer is without an impressive academic résumé.

The announcements completed, the worship begins. Often, it starts in a manner reminiscent of any evangelical megachurch in America: an energetic leader in black jeans and a T-shirt exhorts and shouts for response between lively songs carefully chosen to energize the crowd, drums and bass guitar throbbing. Yet here at Trinity, this continues only for a short while before the choir files in, several hundred strong, and takes the lead. Choir members are dressed in a loosely coordinated African color scheme, each showing individuality and yet connection to the whole in their dress.

The music now ended, a few prayers are voiced; then a young man takes the pulpit. His name is Rev. Otis Moss III, and he is the new lead pastor. Tall and handsome, he is thirty-seven years old, a Yale graduate, and he comes to Trinity from a successful pastorate in Georgia. His oratorical skills are immediately obvious. He speaks in a warm, clipped style that captures both Ivy League and the street; that is, both college professor and black poet. It is easy to understand why the congregation chose this man to guide them for the decades to come.

His sermon is wrapped around the theme of the crucifixion of Jesus, and it is a masterpiece of exposition and tender narrative. He summons characters from history and gives them personality and voice. Cadence and repetition mount, bringing the crowd to its feet often and driving home the central theme. Scholarship—the dissected New Testament Greek word, the patiently explained custom from the time of Jesus, the carefully chosen historical anecdote—merges with a pastor's insight into human nature to craft an impact on the congregation that is at once educational, inspiring, and of unsparing challenge. Few sermons as good will be preached anywhere in America on this Sunday morning.

> Jesus is a "half-naked man of color," who loses His life at the conspiring hands of a corrupt white Italian nation and the coconspirators within His own race.

The outsider, particularly if he is white, will notice two likely unexpected characteristics of the preaching. The first is the altered detail of Bible stories from what he has known. Jesus is a "half-naked man of color," who loses His life at the conspiring hands of a corrupt white Italian nation and the coconspirators within His own race. Probably, the white visitor has never thought of the crucifixion story in this way. The second feature is how at any moment in the sermon, a Bible story might be shifted to its racial or political parallel today. Trumped-up charges against Jesus at the hands of the Pharisees swiftly become the means of understanding how the Los Angeles police plant evidence or how George W. Bush will likely have to place weapons of mass destruction in Iraq where there were none before. These asides excite the crowd as much as the passionate biblical narrative of the sermon, and the visitor notes that even the few white members of the congregation often stand up in support of these moments of political commentary.

Hovering over all is the spirit of a man who is not present, who is only occasionally mentioned, but who nevertheless pervades the whole. He is referred to with honor in nearly every prayer. His name, offered as an aside in an announcement, prompts applause. During the sermon, the difficulties he has endured of late are compared with the sufferings of Jesus and His abuse by both the cowardly religious and the sinfully political. When the sermon concludes with an impassioned description of Jesus being lifted up on the cross, this man is also portrayed as one whose sufferings will allow him to be lifted up and vindicated before a watching world.

His name is Rev. Jeremiah A. Wright Jr., and he has been the senior pastor of this people, until recently, for thirty-six years. When he first became their shepherd in 1972, the congregation numbered only eighty-seven souls but had already found the courage to declare themselves "unashamedly black and unapologetically Christian."

Ablaze with purpose and with his red-tinged Afro nearly a symbol of his passion, Rev. Wright began building in those days what would become a Chicago institution and the largest church of the United Church of Christ denomination.

Now, though, these achievements tend to fade behind the firestorm that has attended the end of his pastoral ministry. For this is the man whose raging statements have been viewed on YouTube hundreds of thousands of times, who has declared that "God damns America," that racism rules the United States—the "U.S.K.K.K.A."—and that the horrors of September 11, 2001, were "America's chickens coming home to roost." And he also is the man who has perhaps become the largest political liability for his spiritual son, Senator Barack Obama.

Ask about the man's character among his congregation, though, and a different picture forms. A deacon recalls when Dr. Wright spoke at a struggling church nearby and afterward refused his honorarium, insisting that instead the money be used for the church's meager building fund. An older woman recalls traveling to Africa with her pastor and noticing the tears in his eyes as he taught about the motherland of his race. Then there are tales of the tender reminiscences of childhood that fill his sermons, of the pastoral gentleness of his visits to troubled homes and of his generosity in a poor community.

Older men cackle as they recall Rev. Wright's humor—and his strong language. He is known for lacing his sermons with the vocabulary of the street. A visiting minister to Trinity recently found himself at a point in his sermon where he shouted the word "No!" as part of a story. Then, pausing, he said instead, "Hell, no!"

With a smile, he explained, "Jeremiah Wright taught me that." The crowd erupted in knowing laughter. Dr. Wright might be a "cussin' preacher," but he's their preacher, and they love him.

Wright was born in 1941 to a Baptist pastor's home in Philadelphia. The son and grandson of ministers, he enrolled as a freshman at the historically black Virginia Union University when he was eighteen. Before he finished his degree, though, he left the school to join the U.S. Marines. Stories vary as to why. The nobler version is that he was inspired by John F. Kennedy's "Ask not what your country can do for you" speech and gave up his student deferment to serve his country. The more likely reason is that he became disenchanted with Christianity's weak support for the civil rights movement and lost interest in a pastoral calling. Whatever the cause, he served in the Second Marine Division and then transferred into the Navy. He returned to college in 1967 when he enrolled in historically black Howard University in Washington, D.C., earning a bachelor's degree and a master's degree in English

There was turmoil beneath the surface of this journey. Wright, characteristically, tells the story, sparing nothing. At Virginia Union, he had begun to see "the underside (or the seedy side) of the Black church and hypocritical Black preachers."[2] This disillusionment paralleled the rise of the civil rights movement. Wright participated in sit-ins and resisted "the 'honkies' I was growing to hate with each passing day."[3] Bluntly, he says, "[in those days I] was singing as a soloist in the traveling university choir, getting drunk for the first time in my life, and trying to sort out my call to ministry."[4]

His mentor was Dr. Samuel Proctor, a professor he met at Virginia Union and a leading black educator who served also at North

Carolina A&T and Rutgers University. Wright remembers that at the time, Proctor "produced more African American PhDs at Rutgers than any other person in the history of the school."[5] More important for the man Wright would become, "Proctor was always pointing me to a higher calling and a deeper commitment to a faith grounded in a carpenter from Capernaum who knew oppression, who knew hatred and who knew colonialism, but who also knew (personally) a God who was greater than any government and who promised a peace more powerful than any peace the 'world' could ever give."[6] With Proctor's encouragement, Wright reclaimed his sense of calling to ministry and began to prepare by earning a master's at the University of Chicago Divinity School and later a doctorate at United Theological Seminary.

As he stepped into ministry, he was fully aware of the crisis of faith in the black community. Blacks were leaving the Christian church in the 1970s for other religious traditions that seemed to belong more naturally to the black experience. The Nation of Islam and the Black Hebrew Israelites, among others, thrived as a result. "They didn't know African-American history," Wright insists. "They were leaving churches by the boatloads. The church seemed so disconnected from their struggle for dignity and humanity."[7] About this time Wright accepted the lead role at Trinity United Church of Christ.

He would build at Trinity on the foundation of a new black theology, one that began to emerge in the late 1960s to fierce controversy. Wright would insist, though, that this theology—the Christianity that arises organically from the black experience, that in fact *is* the black experience—did not originate in the 1960s or even in America. It was fashioned, he would preach, in the struggles of the Old Testament people of God and through the birth of a New Testament faith. It was hammered out on the anvil of the trans-Atlantic slave trade and systematized by black thinkers and theologians for generations before finding its public voice in the crises of race that attended the troubled decade of the 1960s in America. It was the theology, he would proclaim, of a people determined to be subjects in history, not objects.

The symbolic call to arms of this black theology may have been sounded on July 31, 1966, when fifty-one black pastors took out a full-page ad in the *New York Times* demanding results in eradicating racism. The age was in turmoil, and the black church was beginning to engage—and engage aggressively. A manifesto issued by a gathering of black theologians in Atlanta three years later ended with Eldridge Cleaver's battle cry: "We shall have our manhood. Or the earth will be leveled by our efforts to gain it." The killing of their leaders and the suffering that plagued their communities were too much to tolerate in silence any longer. Though the black churches came late to the battle for social equality— Martin Luther King Jr. had been kicked out of his denomination just years before for the "excesses" of his political activism—when they finally took up the challenge, they did so with a vengeance.

In 1969, theologian James Cone issued the Magna Carta of black theology, a work called *Black Theology and Black Power*. Influenced by Stokely Carmichael's black power ideology, Malcolm X's intellectual taunts of white Christianity, and Martin Luther King Jr.'s demand for civil rights, Cone built a theology of and for the black experience. At the heart of this theology was the idea of liberation. Since Jesus described Himself as a liberator—whose task was to "preach good news to the poor . . . to proclaim freedom for the prisoners . . . to release the oppressed"[8]—the work of the church now ought to be the same.

This core idea sounds Christian enough, but Cone came to emphasize this matter of liberation nearly to the exclusion of all other biblical doctrines. On the matter of revelation, for example, he maintained that revelation only occurs where God enters history to liberate the oppressed from their oppressors. That was a break from the traditional perspective that God speaks through Scripture, by the Holy Spirit, and through the anointed leaders of His church. Now, with Cone, liberation became both the means and the moment of revelation. "In a word," Cone argued, "God's revelation means liberation—nothing more, nothing less."[9]

Cone also insisted that all who suffer oppression are "black," no matter their skin color. Being black meant taking the side of the oppressed against the oppressor. So when Cone proclaimed that Jesus is black, that whites want Christianity without blackness, and that the Scriptures can be interpreted only by blacks, he was issuing a call to reinterpret Christianity in terms of its lost themes of suffering and liberation, yet he was using language that assured resistance from both white and traditional black churches. In this sense, the black experience became ultimate for Cone:

> I still regard the Bible as an important source of my theological reflections, but not the starting point. The black experience and the Bible together in dialectical tension serve as my point of departure today and yesterday. The order is significant. I am black

first—and everything else comes after that. This means that I read the Bible through the lens of a black tradition of struggle and not as the objective Word of God. The Bible therefore is one witness to God's empowering presence in human affairs, along with other important testimonies.[10]

The corollary is, of course, that whiteness is oppression, that whiteness is slavery, that whiteness is power in opposition to the very thing that Jesus Christ came to do.

Even for those who understood Cone's language—Jesus is a "black" man come to destroy "white" systems of oppression—his message was radical and often violent. A typical sentence from his *A Black Theology of Liberation* reveals the sentiments that enraged white readers and thrilled many black activists: "Black theology must realize that the white Jesus has no place in the black community, and it is our task to destroy him."[11] Similarly, "black theology is concerned only with the tradition of Christianity that is usable in the black liberation struggle."[12] Or, "for too long Christ has been pictured as a blue-eyed honky. Black theologians are right; we need to dehonkify him and thus make him relevant to the black condition."[13] These statements were troubling enough to the society of the day, yet there were others that seemed designed to set a match, almost literally, to the tinderbox of animosity: "The black experience is the feeling one has when attacking the enemy of black humanity by throwing a Molotov cocktail into a white-owned building and watching it go up in flames. We know, of course, that getting rid of evil takes something more than burning down buildings, but one must start somewhere."[14]

In the eyes of most traditional churches, both black and white, Cone was simply mixing Christianity with Marxism. He was remaking Jesus into a "People's Messiah" who preached a message of political liberation rather than spiritual regeneration. Accordingly, some feared, a black man might shoot a white man or burn down a white-owned business and believe himself to be doing the will of Jesus Christ, the Prince of Peace. The same Jesus who told His disciples not only to love all nations but also to teach them to do His will was being presented as a "whitey-hating" black man come to destroy all but black society. Evangelical scholar Francis Schaeffer had written that "liberalism is nothing more than humanism in theological clothing," leading Cone's evangelical critics to conclude that black theology was little more than black bigotry reworking the mission of Jesus.

Radical or not, violent or not, Cone's vision launched a generation of black ministers, and Jeremiah Wright was among them. He became an expert in black theology, not only as Cone taught it but also as other theologians rearticulated and extended it. Taking the lead at Trinity United Church of Christ in 1972, just as black theology was filling its sails with the winds of the age, Wright began preaching his theology of liberation to the oppressed people on Chicago's South Side. It was refreshing to their souls: a strengthening of their hopes in God, a confirmation of their political suspicions, a celebration of their history, an affirmation of the goodness of their race, and an arming for the cultural battles to come.

Through the years, the people of Trinity Church were exposed to a view of the United States far different not only from that taught in the nation's schools, but also from that preached to most black congregations and in most suburban churches of the country. For black people—both black in skin color and "black" as the oppressed—American history as Wright taught it was no longer a noble tale of the advancement of freedom. White Americans might get misty-eyed at the remembrance of Jamestown as the first permanent English settlement on the shores of the New World, but for blacks, Jamestown was where American slavery began in 1619. White Americans could boast of their intrepid founding fathers, but blacks at Trinity Church were urged to remember a compromising generation who spoke movingly of human equality yet who extended slavery. Let politicians tell lies about the glories of World Wars I and II, Wright would insist, but blacks should recall Jim Crow laws and a segregated army that only begrudgingly tolerated the black flying aces of Tuskegee. Having determined to see the world in terms of the oppressors and the oppressed, Wright found America on the oppressor side almost every time.

> Black theology shaped Wright's understanding of the world and America's role in it. The U.S. bombings of Hiroshima and Nagasaki were never bold, ingenious ends to a bloody war. They were massacres of a people of color by a white nation.

Black theology shaped Wright's understanding of the world and America's role in it. The U.S. bombings of Hiroshima and Nagasaki were never bold, ingenious ends to a bloody war. They were massacres of a people of color by a white nation.

America's support for Israel? No less than white imperialists oppressing a Palestinian people of color through a client state. America's post-9/11 war in Afghanistan and Iraq? Merely a tyrannical nation sending her people of color to colonize yet another people of color for little more than oil. So it would be with South Africa, Grenada, Native Americans, women, Bosnia, Somalia, Vietnam, gays, lesbians, and immigrants. Jesus came to liberate the downtrodden, and Jeremiah Wright would be His disciple, supporting the oppressed wherever they were to be found in the world.

His views set him in tension not only with many in white America but even with some of his fellow black churchmen. He stood for abortion rights, against school prayer, and for laws protecting gays and lesbians. He urged the U.S. government to pay reparations to blacks for slavery and to pour more foreign aid into Africa. He raged against the "prosperity gospel" of black and white churches and thought nothing of accusing a fellow pastor of promoting a "pimp theology for a prostituted church." His views flew hard and fast on the wings of his astonishing oratorical gifts, and he was not afraid to depart from any text in any sermon to expound on the evils of his society or his race.

Often of surprise to white observers, Wright did not simply wait for the U.S. government to fund the liberation of his people. Indeed, the notorious sermon in which he proclaimed that "God damns America" was titled "Confusing God and Government," a call to cease looking to government to fulfill the promises of God. Wright was not waiting for a government check. During his years at Trinity, he preached the values of black self-sufficiency and, despite his pastoral load, helped start corporations to bring prosperity to the people in his community. He also raged against the insular values of a black middle class, of a people who had just enough to inoculate them against concern for others. He challenged both the wealthy and the poor of his congregation to give—and give radically—for the cause of Jesus in the world.

This, then, was Jeremiah Wright: brilliant, angry, successful, and unapologetic—passionate for his people, passionate for his Christ, and passionate to understand the world in exclusively liberation terms. And his critics raged. He was a "demonized man," "anti-Semitic," "a Communist fellow traveler," and "a racist." He was perceived to be the epitome of the problem with black leadership in America, a cult leader of heretical views.

Yet while his critics spewed, his influence and following grew. There seemed to be no middle ground in public opinion. Jeremiah Wright was either demon or deliverer.

The truth is that he was, and is, a conundrum, hard to reconcile, a mixture of greatness and grief. He could lead thousands to faith and then spout urban myth as gospel. He could proclaim the "old, old story" of Christian truth and the latest conspiracy theories in nearly the same breath. He could bitterly rail against his nation and yet be, as he was, the most respected black preacher of spiritual revival in the country. He could lead a people to holiness and swear like a gangbanger in the pulpit. He could be generous and small, ennobling and crushing, glorious and dark.

Then there were stories like this one that only extended the mystery. William A. Von Hoene Jr. was a white man in love with a black woman. She was a member of Trinity Church and an activist in the cause of her people. She was also in love with William—and deeply troubled by it. How could she marry a white man and keep respect in her black community? Wouldn't a white husband undermine all she hoped to accomplish for her race? So in her torment, she broke off her engagement to William.

Jeremiah Wright heard about her crisis. He called her, asked her to "drop everything" to meet with him, and then spent four hours pouring out his heart. God does not want us to make decisions about people based on race, he told her. The future

> *Yet while Wright's critics spewed, his influence and following grew. There seemed to be no middle ground in public opinion. Jeremiah Wright was either demon or deliverer.*

belongs to those who are prepared to break down barriers. Racial divisions aren't acceptable, no matter the pain that caused them. Marry this man, he told her, and forge a new history together. And a few months later, Rev. Jeremiah Wright performed the ceremony in which the white William married his African-American bride.[15]

This from the racist pastor of Trinity United Church of Christ. This from the man who damns America in the name of God. This from the scholar who claims that Jesus is black. And all of this, the angry and the kind, the holy and the harsh, would come to bear on the life of Barack Obama.

The Sunday morning service at Trinity United Church of Christ has dismissed, and the visitor makes his way to the door. Walking out into the biting Chicago air, he falls in with the departing crowd to greetings exchanged through scarves and gloved hands.

The visitor finds himself behind a mother and her son. He has seen these two earlier that morning walking their half mile to church against the cold.

"Momma, do you wanna hear what I learned this morning?"

"Yes, baby. Tell me"

"I learned that the man who helped Jesus carry the cross was from Africa. He was prob'ly black."

"That's right, baby. What else did you learn?"

"Teacher also told us that some of the men at Antioch, where they sent out Paul and *Billabus* to be missionaries, some of those men were black like you and me too."

"It's Barnabas, honey, but that's right. One of those men's names even means 'black man.'"

"That's right, Momma. And did you know that there was an *unchun* from Ethiopia? He's in the Bible and he was black too."

"Baby, you say that word *eunuch*, but you are so right. That man was a black man from Africa. I'm so proud of you knowing that."

"I know, Momma. I can't wait to tell 'em at school. I bet they don't know it."

The visitor, having heard, begins to understand. And though he is white and of another theological stream, he looks back at Trinity United Church of Christ and sees it for a moment through different eyes, and as though for the first time.

3

Faith Fit for the Age

MEN FIND GOD IN VARYING WAYS, EVEN WITHIN THE Christian fold. For most, faith comes in a progression, through a layering of truth over time. Others grasp God in moments of crisis, in desperation, clenching certainties that sustain them all their lives. Then there are those, a select few, who experience dramatic encounters with God, who glimpse with human eyes the glories of an invisible realm. Truly, religious conversions are as varied as those converted and the ways of Providence in dealing with men. There is no single pattern, no schedule by which to compare. It is the destination that remains firm. The road to faith winds and bends.

The conversion of Barack Obama, too, defies pattern, refuses to fall cleanly between theological lines. Yet his turning to faith was one fit for his age. He came as many of his generation do—not so much to join a tradition as to find belonging among a people; not so much to accept a body of doctrine as to find welcome for what they already believe; not so much to surrender their lives but to enhance who they already are.

We should remember how Obama has described his conversion, the phrases that have played so often in his speeches and books. In *The Audacity of Hope*, he wrote that "it came about as a choice and not an epiphany; the questions I had did not magically disappear. But kneeling beneath that cross on the South Side of Chicago, I felt God's spirit beckoning me. I submitted myself to His will, and dedicated myself to discovering His truth."[1] In later interviews he sometimes used more traditional language. He has, he says, a "personal relationship with Jesus Christ," and he believes "in the redemptive death and resurrection of Jesus Christ" "that faith gives me a path to be cleansed of sin and have eternal life."[2]

At Trinity United Church of Christ, a call to faith, an altar call occurs at the end of most every Sunday service. It follows a now-familiar pattern in American religion. The sermon comes to a close and takes the form of an appeal. Jesus is calling, the crowd is told. As music fills the sanctuary, those who believe God is dealing with them are called to the front. Don't hesitate, the pastor urges; this is about God and you. Forget the crowd, the cameras. Your friends and family will wait. Come do the business your soul yearns to do. Soon, individuals rise from the crowd and make their way to the front. The Trinity staff is prepared for this moment. Ushers walk the aisles, urging the willing to the fore. There, all are greeted by leaders who form the sometimes weeping seekers into a line. The pastor gives gentle words of instruction and offers a prayer for each soul. Then all are moved to another room for counsel. As they go, the congregation applauds and shouts words of support. Many in the crowd have walked that tearful line before.

Obama has recounted that he first met with Jeremiah Wright and then attended Trinity Church in 1985. Before long he heard the transforming "Audacity of Hope" sermon. Yet it was months before he responded to a call to faith, months before he made his way to the front of the room and confessed his faith in Christ. He was likely battling his lifestyle of detachment. It would have been more natural for him to sit and watch but feel himself apart, to protect his heart through distance. The power of Trinity Church wouldn't allow it, though. Then, too, he "felt God's spirit beckoning."[3]

The day came, and when it did, Obama rose after a particularly powerful sermon and made his way to the front, likely with a white-gloved usher at his side. He would have stood in a line and received a prayer and instruction. If he was willing, he would have made his way to a side room where fathers in faith would have helped him find his God.

In early retellings of this story, before the phrases were honed into the literature now so well-known, Obama says that while at the front of the church, "I did not fall out."[4] The phrase has likely been dropped because it is too esoteric, too much part of the black and Pentecostal experience for most Americans to understand. But to "fall out" means to be so overcome by the power of God or conviction that one can no longer stand and thus falls to the ground. When people at Trinity fall out, ministers usually attend them, pray for them while they are prostrate, and then help the groggy converts to their feet after they "come to." Obama would have seen this repeatedly in the months he had attended Trinity. It might have given him pause, made him hesitate in responding before he did. This "falling out" might have been something he hoped to avoid, something he was too self-conscious, too Columbia University, to want to do. But on the day when he risked it to grasp his new faith, the experience did not occur. Perhaps he was relieved.

Critics of Obama and, certainly, of Jeremiah Wright wonder whether anything approximating the traditional Christian gospel is preached at Trinity Church. Wright's political pronouncements have been so radical and his demeanor in YouTube clips so angry that it is hard for some, particularly evangelicals, to accept that the church is anything more than a black Marxist recruitment center. Yet this is part of the sometimes confusing nature of both Wright and his church. Yes, Jesus Christ is offered to sinners as the Son of God who died and rose again. Yes, the church calls men to be saved from death and hell through confessing their wrongs and submitting their lives to a crucified Christ. Yes, this is the "born-again, new birth, blood-washed, Spirit-empowered Christianity" that evangelicals know.

Exactly what Barack Obama experienced and what he under-stood is hard to discern. He does not use the language of the traditional convert to Christianity. He is the product of a new, post-modern generation that picks and chooses its own truth from traditional faith, much as a man customizes his meal at a buffet. Obama does not recount that he felt an emptiness in his soul, was burdened by the weight of his sins, and so responded to the love of Jesus, who promised to save him and remake him in the image of God. This is the language of evangelicalism. He says, instead, that he was seeking a "vessel" for his values, a "community or shared traditions in which to ground my most deeply held beliefs."[5] Rather than yield his mind without reserve to Scripture and its revelation of God, Obama was relieved that a "religious commitment did not require me to suspend critical thinking."[6] Rather than "renounce the world and its ways"—standard Christian language for breaking with the sinful ways of society—he was pleased that his faith would not require "retreat from the world that I knew and loved."[7] Rather than commit to Jesus Christ because of truth he had already found sure, Obama instead admitted, "[The] questions I had didn't magically disappear," and so in conversion he "dedicated [himself] to discovering [God's] truth."[8]

It was language sure to raise doubts. In an age in which a man can easily lose a political race for lack of religious fluency, Obama risked such broad language in describing his conversion that he pleased only those who prefer the matter remain unresolved. Evangelicals were unimpressed. Young postmoderns rejoiced in the mood of spiritual seeking and the ring of honesty in Obama's words. The language was so broad that even the nonreligious weren't offended. Consider John K. Wilson's understanding of Obama's Christ in *Barack Obama: This Improbable Quest*: "For Obama, Jesus isn't a magical creature to be worshipped blindly; he's a real person to be imitated for his moral example. What's important to Obama about Jesus is not the 'Night of the Living Dead' aspects of a Christian belief in a resurrection, but the moral lessons about self-sacrifice for a larger cause."[9] Though this is far from the Christ of Trinity Church, and from what Obama describes in interviews, the portrayal of his conversion in *The Audacity of Hope* is so broad that it does admit such a view.

The uncertainty that Obama's words inspire seems intentional. Though it does not appear that he means to confuse, he does speak with a thoughtful lack of clarity, or perhaps with well-considered doubt, for doubt is at the heart of Obama's religion. Indeed, it is not going too far to say that for Obama, doubt is a form of worship. "I think that religion at its best comes with a big dose of doubt," he explains.[10] His religion is "a faith that admits doubt, and uncertainty, and mystery. Because, ultimately," he says, "I think that's how most people understand their faith. In fact, it's not faith if you're absolutely certain. There's a leap that we all take, and when you admit that doubt publicly, it's a form of testimony."[11] This studied uncertainty permeates all of Obama's faith: "There are aspects of the Christian tradition that I'm comfortable with and aspects that I'm not. There are passages of the Bible that make perfect sense to me and others that I go, 'Ya know, I'm not sure about that.'"[12]

> "There are aspects of the Christian tradition that I'm comfortable with and aspects that I'm not. There are passages of the Bible that make perfect sense to me and others that I go, 'Ya know, I'm not sure about that.'"

Making the nature of Obama's Christian commitment even more difficult to pin down is the way he speaks of other religions. In an early speech that included the now famous lines about his conversion—"beneath the cross on the South Side"—he then exulted, "That's a path that has been shared by millions upon millions of Americans—evangelicals, Catholics,

Protestants, Jews and Muslims alike; some since birth, others at certain turning points in their lives."[13] It was a statement guaranteed to raise questions about his own Christianity. Jews and Muslims don't have evangelical conversion experiences. Undoubtedly, Obama was saying that he had found faith on the South Side of Chicago much as people of other faiths were either born into or eventually discovered the meaning of their own religion. Yet by comparing his conversion to the embracing of non-Christian religions, Obama once again blurred the lines of definition, leaving uncertainty about how he viewed his faith.

This line in his speech was more than an unguarded sentence. Obama does clearly believe that the form of Christianity he committed to at Trinity Church in 1985 is not the only path to God. "I am rooted in the Christian tradition," he has said. Nevertheless, he asserts, "I believe that there are many paths to the same place and that is a belief that there is a higher power, a belief that we are connected as a people."[14] He first saw this broad embrace of faith modeled by his mother. "In our household," he has explained, "The Bible, [t]he Koran, and the Bhagavad Gita sat on the shelf alongside books of Greek and Norse and African mythology. On Easter or Christmas Day my mother might drag me to church, just as she dragged me to the Buddhist temple, the Chinese New Year celebration, the Shinto shrine, and ancient Hawaiian burial sites."[15] What his mother sought to embed in him was her view that "underlying these religions was a common set of beliefs about how you treat other people and how you aspire to act, not just for yourself, but also for the greater good." Thus, for Obama, Christianity is but one religious tree rooted in the common ethical soil of all human experience.

> "I am rooted in the
> Christian tradition,"
> he has said.
> Nevertheless, he
> asserts, "I believe
> that there are many
> paths to the same
> place and that is a
> belief that there is a
> higher power, a belief
> that we are connected
> as a people."

This foundation of doubt and a Christianity taken as but one of many paths to God overlay even his most casual discussions of faith. Every statement seems a mixture, not only in the sense that it departs from traditional language, but in that there is a joining of disparate themes. Asked by a reporter about his prayer life, Obama spoke of "an ongoing conversation with God," but then suggested that this conversation is actually with himself: "I'm constantly asking myself questions about what I'm doing, why I am doing it."[16] Such an answer admits wide interpretation. Wilson, for example, insists that Obama's prayer life "is not a delusional belief that a supernatural being is talking directly to him. Instead, Obama uses God as a way to check his own ego. He uses prayer to 'take stock' of himself and maintain his 'moral compass.'"[17] Members of Obama's church might be surprised by this conclusion, but Wilson's view is again understandable given the expansive language used by Obama.

This murkiness extends to Obama's view of the afterlife as well. When his daughter once asked him about what happens after death—"I don't want to die, Daddy," he recalls her saying—he was unable to assure her about heaven: "I wondered if I should have told her the truth, that I wasn't sure what happens when we die, any more than I was sure of where the soul resides or what existed before the Big Bang."[18] He also isn't sure about the traditional view of eternal punishment: "I find it hard to believe that my God would consign four-fifths of the world to hell."[19] This leads Wilson to conclude that the "afterlife is neither believed nor disbelieved by Obama; it's ignored because it's an unknowable factor that shouldn't affect what we do on earth."[20]

This view, of course, is deeply disturbing to more traditional, orthodox Christians, for certainty about an afterlife is one of the cardinal doctrines of Christianity, regarded by believers as one of the chief blessings of faith in Jesus Christ. Obama's own church lists heaven among the benefits of salvation in the altar calls that close its services. This is not merely the insistence of evangelicals; this is a central truth of the New Testament. Here too, though, in his view of the Bible, there is evidence of the postmodern picking and choosing. Asked by a reporter how he can so warmly embrace non-Christian faiths when Jesus Christ said, "I am the way, the truth and the life. No one comes to the Father but by me," Obama insisted that this is only a "particular verse" and that its meaning depends on how the few words are interpreted.[21] Similarly, in his support of civil unions for homosexuals, he is not "willing to accept a reading of the Bible that considers an obscure line in Romans to be more defining of Christianity than the Sermon on the Mount."[22] Such statements rankle defenders of traditional Christianity, though, for the Bible itself claims that all its words are "given by inspiration of God" and are "profitable for doctrine."[23] Historically, Christians have believed that no one verse can be set against another to prove it untrue.

What did Barack Obama become, then, on that Sunday morning

in 1985? He became, he says, a Christian. He confessed his faith in Jesus Christ as the Son of God who died for his sins and rose again. Yet he denies that his Christianity is the sole path to God, and he applies a great deal of doubt to the doctrines of his faith: the inspiration of Scripture, the matter of the afterlife, the moral standards of tradition. In this he is not alone. His Christianity is shared by most of the mainline Protestant denominations today as well as the unchurched young in America, who rework traditional faith in their generational image.

> In his support of civil unions for homosexuals, he is not "willing to accept a reading of the Bible that considers an obscure line in Romans to be more defining of Christianity than the Sermon on the Mount."

We should draw conclusions cautiously, though. All faith is a work in progress, and no man can be accurately portrayed by a portrait frozen in time. At the very heart of Obama's belief is a "Living Word of God" that ever reveals and expands, that comes from unexpected sources. As he wrote in The Audacity of Hope, "When I read the Bible, I do so with the belief that it is not a static text but the Living Word and that I must be continually open to new revelations—whether they come from a lesbian friend or a doctor opposed to abortion."[24] If there is anything certain about Obama's faith in the years to come, it is that there will be an unfolding, an evolving. Given his faith in a "Living Word," "revelation" may very well come to him from the most uncommon and unlikely sources. Yet it will come, for religiously, Barack Obama is not now what he will be—as certainly as he is not now what he was the day before that transforming Sunday in 1985.

The most pressing concern for most Americans, though, is not so much Obama's postmodern Christianity, but his more than two decades at Trinity United Church of Christ. The images live too vividly in the popular mind to ignore. Jeremiah Wright's heated exchange with Sean Hannity of Fox News. The sermon in which America is damned for her racism. The insistence that HIV/AIDS is a weapon devised by the U.S. government to be used against blacks. The claim that America is an oppressive empire not unlike ancient Rome. The unswerving support for the Palestinian cause. The declaration that the sufferings of September 11, 2001, are the fruits of America's national sins, of her chickens coming home to roost.

That Jeremiah Wright, noted African-American leader, holds these views is offensive enough to many Americans. That Barack Obama, a U.S. senator, felt comfortable sitting under his ministry for two decades is even more troubling, if polls are to be believed. The critical question, then, is why did Obama stay, not just for some twenty years, but even after his pastor's radical views became public?

He admits that his first forays into the world of Trinity were pragmatic. Friends told him that his work in the South Side community would go better if people saw him in church, if they knew where he got his faith. Obama took this as true. It also could not have escaped his notice that attending Trinity was a wise political move. A big, visible church where many upwardly mobile and politically active blacks attended was just the place he wanted to be. He did not deceive himself about this motive for attending church, nor did he fail to admit to it later in life.

Yet once he began to visit the church, all the evidence indicates that he was genuinely captured by the experience. It is significant that, years later, when his connection to Trinity came into question, Obama listed among his reasons for staying that "Rev. Wright preached the gospel of Jesus."[25] It may have been, in part, just that simple. He had come to Trinity with a restless heart, yearning for what the skepticism and the atheism of his upbringing could not provide. Rev. Wright's more strident pronouncements aside, the compassion and mercies of Jesus Christ were tenderly preached in Obama's hearing. He would be assured that Jesus, ever the Liberator, was first the Savior who called men to acknowledge Him as God and to welcome His sacrifice for sin. In time, Obama would make this Savior his own. Thus, he would confirm the truth of Saint Augustine, an African church father of the fourth century, who once wrote, "You have formed us for yourself, and our hearts are restless till they find their rest in you." Obama had found the answer for his soul's need, and only a cynical heart would refuse the possibility of a lonely black man in his twenties finding faith through the preaching of God's Word.

At Trinity he also found affirmation and celebration of his African heritage. His exotic background had long been a source of conflict for him. He knew few who were like him and spent much of his youth explaining how he was African, but not really African-American, and how he wasn't really either one because his mother was white. Trinity brought an end to the struggle. Each Sunday—in the dress of his fellow church members, in the Pan-African flag at the front of the church, in the songs and the sermons that he heard—Africa, land of his father, was honored. Rev. Wright led tour groups to Africa almost every year, invited African Christians to preach in Trinity's pulpit, presented the Bible as truth sprung from African soil, and did all he could to bring glowing honor to the motherland of his race. This ennobled Obama, healed him, fine-tuned his sense of himself, and gave him belonging he had seldom known.

There was, too, the political vision of his newfound church. Had Obama attended another church, he might have heard Christianity preached as a retreat from reality, as a spiritual quest divorced from the world. At still another, he might have been urged to merely seek personal prosperity as a sign of God's approval and grace. Instead, he planted himself at Trinity under Jeremiah Wright and found theological sanction for his political liberalism. Remember that as Obama investigated Trinity Church, he was looking for a "vessel" for values he already had, for "community or shared traditions in which to ground [his] most deeply held beliefs."

He found it. Trinity was activist, politically liberal, and preached a view of Scripture that rooted individual faith in an obligation to change the world. Through the Liberation Theology of Jeremiah Wright, this meant sanction for political views and passions that Obama yearned to connect to a bedrock of faith. That he was pro-choice was clearly the will of God, according to Wright, for it meant he spoke in defense of the rights of women. That he strongly supported a wide separation between church and state served the vision of keeping the oppressor's hands off the pulpits of the land, of keeping "white" religion from grasping the controls of power. That he spoke in the cause of criminals or immigrants or homosexuals or the poor only meant he was following in the footsteps of Jesus, the Liberator, the "black Jesus" who came to destroy the "white Jesus" of the age.

Obama would also find at Trinity encouragement for his intellectual and professional quest. It is not a coincidence that he attended Harvard, practiced law, ran for public office in Illinois, and sought the presidency all after his connection to Trinity began. Trinity called for people to rise, created an environment of learning and achievement, and modeled the pursuit of intellectual excellence. Another pastor might joke about a seminary being a cemetery and about how believers could "get their learning and lose their burning." Jeremiah Wright, a man with four earned degrees, used, as Obama later wrote, "twenty-five-cent words" with regularity. He hired only well-educated staff, put university professors in charge of Sunday school classes, and worked to send the youth of his church to the most reputable schools in the land. Understanding a single Jeremiah Wright sermon might require knowing something of Middle East history, Greek, Hebrew, the amendments to the U.S. Constitution, the causes of World War II, the politics of the Sudan, and the details of how syphilis is spread. Obama thrived in such an environment. It fueled his intellectual curiosity, answered his theological questions, and honored his intention to rise on the strength of his mind.

As much as any other good that Trinity offered Obama, it gave him a place to belong. Though he came to faith as a man, he carried the soul of a boy who yearned for a father and a tribe to call his own.

Trinity answered that need. Jeremiah Wright became his spiritual father, and the church became a bighearted family of a kind he had never known. In approaching the Barack Obama story preoccupied with politics and race, some neglect to understand the simple joys that Trinity offered him. There were hugs and meals and stories to be shared. Rev. Wright could wring a laugh from a crowd that would live for weeks, and no one enjoyed it more than Obama. There were small-group gatherings, basketball games, and meals to be carried to the sick. There were also holy rituals to mark the times of life and sacred ceremonies to define the seasons of the year. Obama put down roots in this welcoming soil. He was baptized and married there. He dedicated his children there and invested his money and his time. He belonged. Indeed, Trinity is the longest-lasting connection of his life, his only spiritual home and arguably the most defining relationship he has ever known.

He initially stayed. Even after the sermons of Jeremiah Wright embarrassed him and damaged his presidential campaign. When the press was circling and he found himself in the political cross-fire because of another man's extremes. He stayed because he had found a faith, a people, the vessel for belief that he had longed for. He stayed because Trinity became the font of his political vision and gave him the religious framing for his sense of professional calling. But there was more, and it helps answer more fully the question that many have been asking: Why, didn't he immediately walk away when the firestorm over Wright arose?

He thought about it, and once spoke to another upscale, large church pastor about making a switch. But he stayed because by the time of the crisis, he had more than two decades of history at Trinity, and belonging to a people had become everything to him. He stayed because he had seen his daughters grow up as proud granddaughters of Africa, something he knew another church might not produce. He stayed because he had learned to "eat the chicken and spit out the bones," to listen to a sermon carefully and distinguish between the revelation of God and the personality of a man. He stayed because you don't abandon family; you can't leave your spiritual father by the side of the road for the varmints and the thieves. He stayed, too, because he largely agreed with Wright—not with the high-flying, angry rhetoric but with the underlying cause of blacks in the world and the righteous work of setting the oppressed free. And he stayed because, as he said in his speech explaining it all to an unforgiving world, "I can no more disown him than I can disown the black community." What more could he do? This was his father. This was his tribe. How could he walk away?

And yet the day of separation came. It came because Rev Wright made it clear he cared more about the cause of black theology than the political aspirations of his spiritual son. It came because Wright seemed to delight in provoking the press with his antics, his much-ridiculed National Press Club speech on April 28, 2008, a prime example. It came because during the heated battles of Obama's president campaign even guest speakers at Trinity, like Roman Catholic priest Father Michael Phleger, strutted and spouted political venom. And it came, surely, because Obama could see his Republican opponents coming for him and knew his association with Trinity and Wright would be ground zero for a right wing attack. And when it came, it came with sadness, with grief for the loss of years and the pain that politics presses into private life. But it came, nonetheless, this separation, leaving a void and a wound that likely will never fully leave the life of Barack Obama.

His association with Wright aside, there are some cautions suggested by Obama's years at Trinity. Even for those who embrace his postmodern faith and political views, there may still be some reason for concern. For instance, he can clearly be at home with anti-American sentiment. Though he says that he was not present for the more extreme statements by Wright and that he "vehemently condemns" them—there is still no escaping that he has sat under the ministry of a man who publicly rages against his nation, who holds his country in disregard. Has this planted disrespect for country in Obama's soul? Critics suspect so, and they point to his refusal to wear an American flag lapel pin, the many pictures of him on the Internet without his hand on his

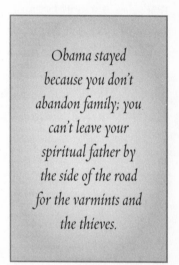

Obama stayed because you don't abandon family; you can't leave your spiritual father by the side of the road for the varmints and the thieves.

heart during the national anthem, and even his wife's statement that "For the first time in my adult lifetime, I am really proud of my country," all to suggest that he is conflicted about his nation. His defenders reject these concerns as petty, but this question can be answered only with the evidence of a deep patriotism on his part over a period of years.

There is also the fear that Obama is too comfortable with Islam, that his years at Trinity have led him to see it not as the basis of a threat but as the faith of an oppressed people, as merely an alternate route to God. Jeremiah Wright earned a master's degree in Islamic studies. He has long supported and befriended the controversial Black Muslim leader Louis Farrakhan, has traveled with him to Africa, and has made friends with numerous Islamic leaders in the Middle East. Members of Trinity have opened their Sunday bulletins to find articles written by Palestinian advocates. Obama has made his spiritual home in this environment, and it is not mere bigotry to ask if it has made him predisposed to a faith that at its radical edge poses the direst threat to America. This is not in the same league of silliness and insult as paying undue attention to Obama's middle name—Hussein—or wondering if he is a Muslim Manchurian candidate sent to subvert the American government. It is a question that his connection to Trinity raises and of which even the most understanding observer of his life might well be unsure.

> *To be a member of a church is not necessarily to descend into mindlessness, and a mind as fine as Obama's is less likely to accept ideas unexamined than most.*

In addition to these concerns, there will be falsehoods that surface from Obama's ties to Trinity. Among them is that he is anti-Semitic. Perhaps surprisingly, the opposite is true. He is a strong supporter of Israel, having been influenced by his many Jewish friends in Chicago. Indeed, some Christian friends wish for a more balanced view of the Israeli-Palestinian conflict on his part and cite his lack of experience in the region as one reason for his limited understanding.[26] Still, it would be natural to expect a less pro-Israeli stand from a man mentored by an ally of Farrakhan, from a man whose spiritual father supports the Palestinian cause with zeal.

That this is not the case should inspire caution in making assumptions about what Trinity might have produced in Obama. To be a member of a church is not necessarily to descend into mindlessness, and a mind as fine as Obama's is less likely to accept ideas unexamined than most. That Obama took a public stand when faced with Wright's diatribes—proclaiming that "I vehemently disagree and strongly condemn the statements," that he was "pained and angered" by them—is evidence that not everything Wright taught took root in Obama's life

Neither Obama's conversion nor his years at Trinity would be of such importance, though, were it not for his belief that faith ought to influence governance, that religion has a legitimate role in the marketplace of political ideas. This is not only significant as a break from the traditional secularism of the political Left, but it is critical given the unique religious values Obama carries with him into the political sphere. It is a commitment that has thrust him into heated political battles, forced him into painful soul-searching, and lifted him to the fore of a new brand of faith-based politics, as we shall see.

Ann Dunham with her son, Barack. "For all her professed secularism," Obama has written, "my mother was in many ways the most spiritually awakened person that I've ever known."

The joy of ocean waves: Barack in the surf near Honolulu.

*Young Barack Obama delights in swinging a baseball bat
during his early years in Hawaii.*

*A Happy Child: A perpetually smiling Barack reflects
the contentment of his young life in the early 1960s.*

Barack is embraced by his biological father at the Honolulu Airport in the early 1970s. This was the last time Barack met the man whose name he bore.

Barack, his mother, Ann, and his sister, Maya, sit with Lolo Soetoro, who took the family to Indonesia and then taught young Barack his broad, syncretistic form of Islam.

*Stanley and Madelyn Dunham embrace a teenage Barack.
Their love, their faith, and their idiosyncrasies would
lastingly impact his life.*

*Barack as a student at Columbia University,
exploring the glories of New York City.*

"We worship an awesome God in the Blue States":
The 2004 Democratic Party Convention speech that started it all.

"I can no more disown him than I can disown the black community":
Barack Obama and the Reverend Jeremiah Wright Jr.

*Natasha and Malia Ann Obama with their parents,
Barack and Michelle.*

"I am rooted in the Christian tradition": Barack Obama at prayer.

Barack Obama's "improbable quest" leads to the Democratic presidential nomination in 2008.

4

The Altars of State

THE CANDIDATE WAS UNDER ATTACK. THE LONG AND BRUISING campaign had worn away all civility, and the heavy bombardment had begun. Both sides had drawn blood. Both were suffering from the blows. And it was about to get worse.

The candidate's opponent was a much older man who claimed to have religion on his side. He was a preacher, well-known in his day, and eager to bring faith into the fight. The two had clashed some years before, and it had been an ugly, religious brawl. The preacher had won then and planned to now use the same tactics as before.

The candidate was unprepared. The press reported that he was an "infidel," that his wife was a coldhearted Episcopalian, and that he had been heard to say that church members were no better than drunkards. Rumors spread that the candidate did not accept Jesus

Christ or the doctrines of the Christian faith. In fact, sources reported that the candidate had once claimed "Christ was a bastard."

At first the candidate only whimpered. The preacher, he complained, "never heard me utter a word in any way indicating my opinions on religious matters, in his life." Then he attacked his opponent personally, reminding the press that the preacher was unlikable, the kind of man who once attended a church service and afterward complained that a deacon's prayer was so cold that "three prayers like that would freeze hell over."

None of this quelled the storm, and the candidate realized he had to address the questions about his faith directly. It was true, he admitted publicly, that he was not a member of any Christian church. But it was a lie that he had ever spoken against the Scriptures or had expressed disrespect for religion in general. Yes, in his early life he had attacked the supernatural claims of Christianity, but that was then. Now, he could not conceive of supporting a man for office whom he knew to be an enemy of religion. His opponent already knew this, yet circulated lies about him for mere political gain.

The bludgeoning continued. The gashes deepened. Yet, at long last, the candidate won.[1]

He was, though, a wounded victor. The religious pummeling he had endured drew him no closer to God and left him with more doubts and confusion than he had before. How could he embrace the faith of his opponent—a preacher, no less—who dealt in lies and sliced open men's souls merely to win votes?

The passing years alone gave their answer, for with time and distance came healing. The candidate would continue in politics, rising eventually to high office. There would be tragedy: the deaths of sons, a bloody war, and the hardships of life and manhood common to the ages. While still in office, the candidate would find his God and a faith so strong that he offered it to his nation in some of the most tenderly wrenching terms of any statesman in history.

So deep was this change in his soul that on the night he died, he turned to his wife and said that when his service to his country was done, he wanted to go to Jerusalem and walk in the steps of his Master. It was not to be, but the hope—and the faith that fueled this hope—did much to heal his nation.

This infidel? This nonbeliever? This candidate who some said lacked enough faith to warrant public office?

His name was Abraham Lincoln.

On his third meeting with President George W. Bush, Barack Obama found himself on the receiving end of political advice. "You've got a bright future," the president said. "Very bright. But I've been in this town awhile and, let me tell you, it can be tough. When you get a lot of attention like you've been getting, people start gunnin' for ya. And it won't necessarily just be coming from my side, you understand. From yours, too. Everybody'll be waiting for you to slip, know what I mean? So watch yourself."

While Obama was still wondering about the president's warning, Bush seemed to want to explain his sense of connection to the young senator from Illinois.

"You know, me and you got something in common," Bush offered.

"What's that?"

"We both had to debate Alan Keyes. That guy's a piece of work, isn't he?"[2]

It was a sentiment Obama could welcome with a laugh, for he had indeed debated Alan Keyes—and defeated him decisively in his Senate race of 2004. Yet the memory likely made him wince, for the battle between Obama and Keyes for the U.S. Senate became a contest of worldviews, a microcosm of the larger religious issues at play in American politics. The experience was painful, and thrust Obama into a season of soul-searching and intellectual reexamination that tempered the religious sword he would later wield on the national stage.

The battle with Keyes came about through a process that caused some to label Obama "the luckiest politician in the entire fifty states."[3] Upon announcing his candidacy for the Senate, Obama joined a crowded Democratic primary field. Almost immediately, his two strongest opponents sustained fatal political damage: one under charges of improperly bundling campaign contributions and another when details of his divorce showed allegations of spousal abuse. Obama won the primary and then faced Republican Jack Ryan in the general election. As David Mendell has observed in *Obama: From Promise to Power*, Ryan "looked as if he had been ordered from central casting. He was tall, lean, square-jawed, Ivy League-educated and well spoken. After becoming rich in investment banking, he spent a few years teaching in a private high school in Chicago's inner city and articulated a Jack Kemp-esque, pro-business brand of compassionate conservatism."[4]

The looming campaign promised to offer a classic American political fight, made thrilling by the vast gap between the candidates in personality, principle, and money. Yet it was not to be. Weeks into the campaign, details of Ryan's divorce from actress Jeri Ryan became public. The tales of bizarre sexual rituals, of a wife forced into degrading public sex in clubs around the world, was too much for Ryan's "family values" image to sustain. Within weeks, he dropped out of the race, leaving his party in crisis.

Then came Alan Keyes, admittedly dragged into the fray from Maryland by a desperate Illinois GOP scrambling at the last minute to find a viable candidate. Long an articulate voice of conservative values—and with credentials from Harvard, the U.S. Foreign Service, the Reagan administration, and two presidential races—he had acquired a reputation as a speechmaker and debater of both laser precision and poetic sense reminiscent of the black pulpit. He entered the Illinois race largely to advance the conservative agenda. As he explained to a National Public Radio audience, "You are doing what you believe to be required by your respect for God's will, and I think that that's what I'm doing in Illinois."[5]

From the beginning, Keyes faced heated criticism for being a "carpetbagger" because he had never lived in Illinois, he had harshly criticized Hillary Clinton of Arkansas for her Senate run in New

> *As one state senator crassly admitted to Obama, "We got our own Harvard-educated conservative black guy to go up against the Harvard-educated liberal black guy. He may not win, but at least he can knock that halo off your head."*

York—"pure and planned selfish ambition" he called it—and his only property in the state was a rented apartment in downtown Chicago. He had clearly been recruited to counter Obama's star-crossed image. As one state senator crassly admitted to Obama, "We got our own Harvard-educated conservative black guy to go up against the Harvard-educated liberal black guy. He may not win, but at least he can knock that halo off your head."[6]

Obama found Keyes to be a cross between "Pentecostal preacher and William F. Buckley," a man who couldn't "conceal what he clearly considered to be his moral and intellectual superiority."[7] Keyes's soaring oratory and sharp criticism were unapologetically Christian, conservative, and moralistic. He insisted that Obama was encouraging a black genocide by supporting abortion. He alleged that the young state senator evidenced a "breathtaking naiveté" about the Iraq war, displayed "ignorance" of the U.S. Constitution, and endorsed a "hedonistic" gay agenda. Perhaps most injurious, Keyes accused Obama of being a man of faith only "when it's convenient to get votes. At the hard points when that faith must be followed and explained to folks and stood up for and witnessed to . . . he pleads separation of church and state, something found nowhere in the Constitution, and certainly found nowhere in the Scripture as such."[8]

In short, Keyes insisted, "Christ would not vote for Barack Obama because Barack Obama has voted to behave in a way that it is inconceivable for Christ to have behaved."[9] As the *Chicago Tribune* recounted one dramatic moment during a debate, Keyes spread his arms apart and said, "Christ is over here, Senator Obama is over there: the two don't look the same."[10]

This onslaught rattled Obama at first, but he soon recovered. He countered that he didn't need Keyes to lecture him on Christianity: "That's why I have a pastor. That's why I have a Bible. That's why I have my own prayer. And I don't think any of you are particularly interested in having Mr. Keyes lecture you about your faith. What you're interested in is solving problems like jobs and health care and education. I'm not running to be the minister of Illinois. I'm running to be its United States senator."[11]

When Keyes charged that Liberalism is immoral, Obama fired back, "I think there's something immoral about somebody who's lost their job after 20 years, has no health care, or [is] seeing their pension threatened. I think there's something immoral about young people who've got the grades and the drive to go to college but just don't have the money. There are millions of people all across this state that are having a tough time, and Washington is not listening to them, and neither is Mr. Keyes."[12]

It was a faith-based political fight on a grand scale, but Keyes never really had a chance. He was outmanned. He was outspent. He had entered the race far too late. When it was all over, Obama won with a margin of more than 40 percent of the vote. Exit polls showed that while many voters admired Keyes, they thought that his eccentricities—during one interview he inexplicably began singing a Negro

> As Obama later concluded, "Alan Keyes was an ideal opponent; all I had to do was keep my mouth shut and start planning my swearing-in ceremony."

THE FAITH OF BARACK OBAMA

spiritual and during another shocked even Republicans by suggesting tax breaks for all blacks with slave ancestry—made him unfit for office. As Obama later concluded, "Alan Keyes was an ideal opponent; all I had to do was keep my mouth shut and start planning my swearing-in ceremony."[13]

But this flippant dismissal belied the uncertainty that Keyes awakened in Obama's soul. He couldn't move on, couldn't bury Keyes in memory as he had in his landslide political victory. He was still wrestling even months later, as he had been during the campaign, still struggling with what had happened, with the fallout in his own mind from the clash of worldviews that he and Keyes represented.

It galled him that Keyes "claimed to speak for my religion, and my God. He claimed knowledge of certain truths. Mr. Obama says he's a Christian, he was saying, and yet he supports a lifestyle that the Bible calls an abomination. Mr. Obama says he's a Christian, but supports the destruction of innocent and sacred life."[14]

Reflecting on the campaign, Obama knew his answers were stale: "And so what would my supporters have me say? How should I respond? Should I say that a literalist reading of the Bible was folly? Should I say that Mr. Keyes, who is a Roman Catholic, should ignore the teachings of the Pope?" This was a man second-guessing himself, irritated that he had not seized the moment with grace: "Unwilling to go there, I answered with what has come to be the typically liberal response in such debates—namely, I said that we live in a pluralistic society, that I can't impose my own religious views on another, that I was running to be the U.S. Senator of Illinois and not the Minister of Illinois."[15]

But his rhetoric had fallen flat, and he knew it. Even more, he knew he had missed a grand opportunity. The debate between the two eloquent black men "reflected a broader debate we've been having in this country for the last thirty years over the role of religion in politics." This debate raged within Obama as well, and for many months he continued to ponder what had happened in the fall of 2004. By the summer of 2006, he seemed to have settled his mind and resolved his beliefs about faith and democracy. At a conference titled "From Poverty to Opportunity: A Covenant for a New America," sponsored by Jim Wallis's progressive Sojourners organization, Obama gave a speech which not only showed the fruits of his recent soul-searching but also served as a declaration of values for the rising Religious Left.[16]

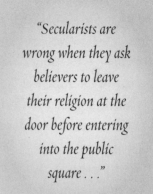

Warning Progressives that "if we don't reach out to evangelical Christians and other religious Americans and tell them what we stand for, then the Jerry Falwells and Pat Robertsons and Alan Keyeses will continue to hold sway," Obama reminded the political Left that in America "90 percent of us believe in God, 70 percent affiliate

"Secularists are wrong when they ask believers to leave their religion at the door before entering into the public square . . ."

themselves with an organized religion, 38 percent call themselves committed Christians, and substantially more people in America believe in angels than they do in evolution."

Then, in a surprising break from the secular legacy of the political Left, Obama charged that "secularists are wrong when they ask believers to leave their religion at the door before entering into the public square . . . to say that men and women should not inject their 'personal morality' into public policy debates is a practical absurdity. Our law is by definition a codification of morality, much of it grounded in the Judeo-Christian tradition."

Progressives, then, should shed their antireligion biases, perhaps finding "some overlapping values that both religious and secular people share when it comes to the moral and material direction of our country. . . And we might realize that we have the ability to reach out to the evangelical community and engage millions of religious Americans in the larger project of American renewal."

This, then, was Obama's message to the political Left: stop rejecting people of faith and instead find common ground. Yet, to the Right, he also offered "some truths they need to acknowledge." First, conservatives, particularly those of the Religious Right, need to recognize the "critical role that the separation of church and state has played" in America. "Whatever we once were," Obama insisted, "we are no longer just a Christian nation; we are also a Jewish nation, a Muslim nation, a Buddhist nation, a Hindu nation, and a nation of nonbelievers."

The paragraph that followed this admonition was one of the most revealing of his speech:

And even if we did have only Christians in our midst, if we expelled every non-Christian from the United States of America, whose Christianity would we teach in the schools? Would we go with James Dobson's, or Al Sharpton's? Which passages of Scripture should guide our public policy? Should we go with

Leviticus, which suggests slavery is okay and that eating shellfish is abomination? How about Deuteronomy, which suggests stoning your child if he strays from the faith? Or should we just stick to the Sermon on the Mount—a passage that is so radical that it's doubtful that our own Defense Department would survive its application? So, before we get carried away, let's read our Bibles. Folks haven't been reading their Bibles.

While insisting on the necessity of the separation between church and state, Obama showed balance, calling for what some termed afterward "First Amendment sanity":

> But a sense of proportion should also guide those who police the boundaries between church and state. Not every mention of God in public is a breach to the wall of separation—context matters. It is doubtful that children reciting the Pledge of Allegiance feel oppressed or brainwashed as a consequence of muttering the phrase "under God." I didn't. Having voluntary student prayer groups use school property to meet should not be a threat, any more than its use by the High School Republicans should threaten Democrats.

In light of American pluralism, then, Obama insisted that religion ought to change its voice when entering the public square. "Democracy demands," he argued:

> that the religiously motivated translate their concerns into universal, rather than religion-specific, values. It requires that their proposals

be subject to argument, and amenable to reason. I may be opposed to abortion for religious reasons, but if I seek to pass a law banning the practice, I cannot simply point to the teachings of my church or evoke God's will. I have to explain why abortion violates some principle that is accessible to people of all faiths, including those with no faith at all.

Finally, and with the taunts of Alan Keyes still vivid in his mind, Obama offered:

I am hopeful that we can bridge the gaps that exist and overcome the prejudices each of us bring to this debate. And I have faith that millions of believing Americans want that to happen. No matter how religious they may or may not be, people are tired of seeing faith used as a tool of attack. They don't want faith used to belittle or to divide. They're tired of hearing folks deliver more screed than sermon. Because in the end, that's not how they think about faith in their own lives.

The speech would prove to be among the most significant of Obama's life. With its tone of moderation, its welcome of faith into the public square, and yet its insistence that people of faith conduct themselves in public debate according to democratic values, it became what Obama had intended: a call to reform, a redefinition of religion's role in American political life. Soon, his words were debated on cable news programs, heard by tens of thousands on YouTube, and argued fiercely on Web sites from every political perspective.

Columnist E. J. Dionne of the *Washington Post* declared that it was "the most important pronouncement by a Democrat on faith and politics since John F. Kennedy's Houston speech in 1960 declaring his independence from the Vatican."[17] Even some conservatives were impressed. Peter Wood of New York's King's College admitted in *National Review* that Obama's "attempt to graft the citrus branch of Christian piety to the hemlock tree of the Democratic Party just might bear fruit."[18]

Thoroughly unimpressed, though, was the secular Left. "More God and country crap from the party that ought to know better," steamed one blogger on a Left-leaning Web site. Believing that religion has no legitimate role in government or public policy, those who embraced a more traditional, secular liberalism could find in Obama's speech little more than betrayal, merely the religious dance now required of politicians in the wake of the Religious Right.

And yet it was from this very Religious Right that the most heated criticism of Obama's speech arose. Though he had tried to address this segment of America—though he had tried to call them to the public square while urging reason and a more democratic tone—Obama's speech only exposed the vast differences between the Religious Right and a newly emerging Religious Left. Understanding these differences, indeed, confronting the fiery opposition of the right in its most full-throated form, is essential to understanding not only some of the battle lines in current American politics but also the religious opposition Obama is likely to face throughout his public career. It is the Religious Right—and its insistence on a political worldview that arises unchecked from Scripture and contends unaltered in the public square—which is Obama's primary intellectual opposition. That Right has been the keeper of the religious flame in

American politics; the primary guardian of a biblically based form of public policy; and the most vocal critic of civil religion, the faith they accuse Obama of fashioning from the secular values of the American way. And that Religious Right suspects the sincerity of Obama's speech, particularly when they consider his response to what is for them the watershed issue of this generation: abortion.

For most religious conservatives, Obama's speech was merely Liberalism repackaged for a new, more faith-sensitive generation. America is no longer a Christian nation, and traditionalists should wake up to the realities of a pluralistic society, they heard Obama saying. No longer are the commands of God welcomed in the public square. Now people of faith must express themselves in something other than "religion-specific values." And that call to "the larger project of American renewal"? That was just Obama's vision for big-government intrusion, a code phrase for the New Frontier and Great Society programs of a new age.

It was true, some admitted, that there had been concessions in the speech to the concerns of traditional Christians. Obama had, after all, rebuked the Left for forcing people of faith to leave their beliefs outside of the public square. He had also conceded that not every public expression of faith violates the separation of church and state. Still, it was not enough, for sounding loud from every page of the speech—as religious conservatives heard it—was an apparent call for traditional Christians to surrender their values, to become "politically correct," in order to be taken seriously by nonbelievers in the nation's public debates. This is what some referred to with sarcasm as Obama's call to join the "American

Church of Pluralism." They meant a temple of state religion in which all faiths are welcome but in which all must bow the knee to an official cult of reason, in which all have a claim, but only if they defer to the religious neutrality of the democratic way.

This charge is critical to understanding how the Religious Right perceives Obama's worldview. Like fiscal conservatives, religious conservatives have long resisted the bloated modern state, yet they have done so for more theological reasons. Religious conservatives warn that the overreaching, intrusive state will not simply silence traditional religions; it will become a religion of its own. This is the tendency of all tyrannical governments, they claim, from ancient Babylon and Rome to Nazi Germany and Stalinist Russia. No one recognized and celebrated this more than the German philosopher Friedrich Hegel, whom conservative scholars from Francis Schaeffer to Michael Novak quote in warning. "The State is the Divine Idea as it exists on earth," Hegel wrote. "We must therefore worship the State as the manifestation of the Divine . . . The State is the march of God through the world."[19]

This view is exactly what alarms religious conservatives. The state as God. American values woven into a religion of its own. Traditional faith kneeling at the altar of the state. The idolatry of an American Shinto. And this is also what they fear in Obama when he declares to a reporter, "Alongside my own deep personal faith, I am a follower, as well, of our civic religion."[20]

> "Alongside my own deep personal faith, I am a follower, as well, of our civic religion."

Conservatives suspect that this "civic religion" is Obama's ploy:

a mask he uses to hide his political and theological liberalism. While sounding the symbolic language of the American experience—"the democratic way," the "neutral public square," "the equality of all religions"—he advances the cause of his old-line, statist liberalism. This civil religion, conservatives would say, is the culturally acceptable language in which he couches his ideals but conceals his agenda. And this is all the more offensive to them because they believe that the very civil religion that Obama would use to replace traditional religion is without any power for solving societal ills. It is, in Will Herberg's oft-quoted phrase, "a religiousness without religion, a religiousness with almost any kind of content or none, a way of sociability or 'belonging' rather than a way of reorienting life to God."[21]

Thus, what Obama's civil religion actually does, some allege, is give people a watered-down religion of Americanism but insulate them from the raw but healing truth of revealed religion. In other words, it replaces traditional religion with a bland political religiosity that creates a mood without offering power. It is merely faith in faith rather than faith in God. As Herbert Schlossberg wrote in *Idols for Destruction*:

A religious statement, on the other hand, which says "do not be conformed to the values of society" swings an axe at the trunk of civil religion. Civil religion eases tensions, where biblical religion creates them. Civil religion papers over the cracks of evil, and biblical religion strips away the covering, exposing the nasty places. Civil religion prescribes aspirin for cancer, and biblical religion insists on the knife.[22]

For the Religious Right, then, civil religion is not unlike Roman emperor Alexander Severus adding Christ to the gods he worshipped in his private chapel. Indeed, civil religion is exactly like President Eisenhower insisting that American government makes no sense "unless it is founded in a deeply felt religious faith—and I don't care what it is."[23] And it is also like Barack Obama using social justice concerns as a call to religious neutrality in honor of the secular American way.

For many evangelicals, Roman Catholics, and religious conservatives, then, civil religion is a kind of idolatry. But they are not surprised to find it coming from Barack Obama. Civil religion, they would argue, is the natural product of Obama's theological liberalism, for when religion is drained of its traditional meaning, it admits to any meaning. That Obama applies the meaning of Scripture to the work of the state, that he calls for a high wall of separation between church and state, and that he insists on the use of nonreligious language in the public square, is exactly what religious conservatives expect. These are tactics to silence the voice of faith, to destroy all gods that compete with the divine state, to demand the surrender of all values inconsistent with the official morality.

Nowhere do religious conservatives find Obama more a shining symbol of this civil religion than in the matter of abortion. This is, in their eyes, the issue that overshadows everything else in American public policy, and largely because abortion as they understand it involves the death of human beings. Initially, they thought Obama might be with them in their views. In his symposium speech, he had said, "I may be opposed to abortion for religious reasons, but if I seek to pass a law banning the practice, I cannot simply point to the teachings of my church or evoke God's will. I have to explain why abortion violates some principle that is accessible to people of all faiths, including those with no faith at all." Some conservatives began to suspect that he might actually believe privately that abortion is the taking of a human life. As he told *Christianity Today*, "I don't know anybody who is pro-abortion."[24]

Yet if he was sensitive to the ambivalence many Americans feel about abortion and the plight of the unborn, his voting record did not show it. As columnist Amanda Carpenter complained in the staunchly conservative *Human Events* some months after Obama's speech, "Senator Barack Obama portrays himself as a thoughtful Democrat who carefully considers both sides of controversial issues, but his radical stance on abortion puts him further left on that issue than even NARAL Pro-Choice America."[25]

> "Barack Obama portrays himself as a thoughtful Democrat who carefully considers both sides of controversial issues, but his radical stance on abortion puts him further left on that issue than even NARAL Pro-Choice America."

Carpenter went on to explain that in 2002, Obama had voted in the Illinois senate against the Induced Infant Liability Act, which would have protected babies who survived late-term abortions. The act sought the same treatment for babies who survived abortions as was routinely provided for babies born premature and thus given lifesaving medical attention. The same year that the

Illinois legislature debated the act, a similar federal bill—called the Born-Alive Infants Protection Act—became law with only fifteen members of the U.S. House opposing it. Indeed, the National Abortion Rights Action League (NARAL), one of the nation's most powerful pro-abortion advocacy organizations, even issued a statement declaring that "NARAL does not oppose passage of the Born Alive Infants Protection Act [because] floor debate served to clarify the bill's intent and assure us that it is not targeted at *Roe v. Wade* or a woman's right to choose."[26] Despite even NARAL having no objection to such bills, Obama voted against the Illinois version in the senate.

Jill Stanek, a registered delivery-ward nurse who became an advocate for the bill after seeing babies born alive and then left to die, testified twice before Obama in support of the bill, as she had earlier before Congress. "I brought pictures in and presented them to the committee . . . trying to show them unwanted babies were being cast aside. Babies the same age were being treated if they were wanted! And those pictures didn't faze [Obama] at all," she remembered.[27]

Transcripts of the hearings reveal that at the end of testimony, Obama thanked Stanek for being "very clear and forthright," but he expressed his concern at Stanek suggesting that "doctors really don't care about children who are being born with a reasonable prospect of life because they are so locked into their pro-abortion views that they would watch an infant that is viable die." Obama concluded, "That may be your assessment, and I don't see any evidence of that. What we are doing here is to create one more burden on a woman and I can't support that."[28]

Obama later explained that he voted against the bill because the language was so broad that it would have disallowed all abortions. Still, the staunchly pro-life Religious Right couldn't understand a man who claimed to be a Christian but voted more pro-choice than even NARAL required. Moreover, as he later admitted, he wasn't sure how his pro-choice politics squared with his faith. "I cannot claim infallibility in my support of abortion rights," he wrote in *The Audacity of Hope.*

> I must admit that I may have been infected with society's predi-
> lections and attributed them to God; that Jesus' call to love one
> another might demand a different conclusion; and that in years
> hence I may be seen as someone who was on the wrong side of
> history. I don't believe such doubts make me a bad Christian. I
> believe they make me human, limited in my understandings of
> God's purpose and therefore prone to sin.[29]

While Obama remained uncertain about abortion, he never-theless voted for babies who survived abortion to then be exposed and left to die. This he did, many of his frustrated critics believed, kneeling before the altar of a "choice at all costs" political correct-ness—under cover of the civil religion that he admits to laying alongside his Christian faith.

Such willingness to surrender faith to politics, as so many of his fellow Christians saw it, brought into question Obama's attempts to heal the nation's religious divide. It defined the dis-tinction in the eyes of the Right between Keyes and Obama, between Jerusalem and Athens, between the bold political vision of Christian founding fathers and the weak, statist theology of a modern civil faith.

Nevertheless, the speech—soon termed the "Call to Renewal" speech—became Barack Obama's religious declaration of intent. If he had summoned the Religious Left in his Democratic National Convention speech of 2004, he gave the movement a blueprint for cultural impact in 2006.

The speech, and the hard-won clarity that produced it, came just in time. Barely six months later, he announced that he was a candidate for the presidency. What followed would prove to be one of the most religiously charged political contests in American history. Yet in the debates, in the "faith forums," in the

> While Obama remained uncertain about abortion, he nevertheless voted for babies who survived abortion to then be exposed and left to die.

controversies that arose from the teachings of his church, and in the taunts from both the Right and the Left, Barack Obama knew who he was religiously, knew what he believed about religion and the state. No more the "typical liberal responses." No more a retreat behind the separation of church and state. Now his worldview was integrated and firm. He was a liberal Christian, embracing a faith-based liberal political vision, and he planned to take both into his nation's corridors of power.

5

Four Faces of Faith

WE LIVE IN A *PEOPLE* MAGAZINE, *INSIDE EDITION*, MEDIA-driven age. The story is the thing, as personal and as detailed as possible. We also live in postmodern times, an age in which what passes for truth comes from the narratives that define our lives. Again, the story is the thing. It is how we apprehend genuineness. Not by exposition and preaching, but by tales well told, by accounts of journeys pregnant with meaning. Story is the medium of our age.

This shapes nothing so much as politics, where a candidate's story becomes cultural icon, where policies are understood to be only as valid as the story of the candidates who proclaim them. There is, in a sense, nothing new here. American history is full of politicians who stretched truth for that "born in the log cabin, up by the bootstraps" narrative. War records were often exaggerated, family embarrassments expunged, and even deformities hidden. Much like today. Yet today technology allows for a multiverse of narrative, of story laid against story in comparison, like so many windows open on a computer screen. Politics becomes the battle of the plotline, the war of story, the competition of the narrative arc.

In a faith-fixated age, this surfaces the tale of the religious journey as well. What has the candidate believed, and how long has he believed it? Was there a conversion, and is there now a tale to be told of a fallen man transformed by grace or goodness or generosity into the shining vision of today? And then, in the one-upsmanship of politics, is Candidate A's faith story superior to Candidate B's? Was there a more dramatic turning? A weightier sense of glory? Stronger evidence by which to know who the anointed really is? This is the cultural dynamic by which the story of Barack Obama's faith is now measured. Already his journey has become, perhaps more than with most politicians, the method of his message. He is the mulatto child born to an atheist home and to a mother whose baby-boomer wanderings sometimes left the family on food stamps. He is the gifted black teenager searching for place and belonging in the exploding cultures of the 1970s. He is a Columbia University graduate working against type in the inner-city neighborhoods of Chicago. He is

> *Fate has landed Barack Obama in a political contest in which all the major candidates, along with the sitting president, represent journeys of faith shared by millions in their generation.*

the godless, aimless one finding Jesus and spiritual home in a church on Chicago's South Side. And he is an astonishingly blessed politician who still walks between worlds—the black and the white, the believing and the secular, the challenged and the privileged, the older generations and the next—giving hope for the healing of our land.

In isolation, his story is a promised coming, a classically American tale reworked for our age. Yet his times demand that his story be held up against the faith stories of others on the national stage, and it is here that we find one of the most defining features of the 2008 presidential election. Fate has landed Barack Obama in a political contest in which all the major candidates, along with the sitting president, represent journeys of faith shared by millions in their generation. Indeed, it is not going too far to contend that the major political players in 2008—Obama, Hillary Clinton, John McCain, and George W. Bush—represent the dominant religious forces in American politics today. They are, then, four faces of the faith of their times, and Obama's story will long be understood in light of—indeed, will long be measured against—these iconic narratives of faith.

The comparison must begin with what has come before, with the faith of the fathers, with a heritage rooted in love of God and country. This is John McCain. Though he is not of the Greatest Generation, who fought World War II and then returned home to refashion their nation, he is of that slightly younger Silent Generation, who were too young to fight their fathers' war but too old and too touched by sacrifice to fit the baby-boomer mold.

McCain was born in 1936 to an esteemed U.S. Navy family, to a culture shaped by the Naval Academy and the call of a nation in crisis. Among his earliest memories was the Japanese bombing of Pearl Harbor. Among his earliest impressions was the inconsistent reality of his father's faith and his father's drinking. In his autobiographical *Faith of My Fathers*, McCain wrote, "My father didn't talk about God or the importance of religious devotion. He didn't proselytize. But he always kept with him a tattered, dog-eared prayerbook, from which he would pray aloud for an hour, on his knees, twice every day." Then the very next sentence of McCain's recollection is that "he drank too much, which did not become him. And I often felt that my father's religious devotion was intended in part to help him control his drinking."[1]

Here is one of the keys to understanding the faith of John McCain. From his father's generation he came to understand religion as the power behind character, as the fuel of right behavior. This observation is to take nothing from that generation's devotion to God, but to say that the primary expression of that devotion was understood to be character and duty, the virtues of a people informed by faith. McCain welcomed this vision of conduct as the principal fruit of faith and made it his own.

It was easy for him, then, to merge devotion to God into a code that also served his country's call to arms. A man served his God by offering his life on the altar of obedience. He served his country in much the same way. Both led to a life of self-sacrifice, of hardship nobly endured, of devotion to a higher cause. As McCain himself summarized the lessons of his early life, "To sustain my self-respect for a lifetime it would be necessary for me to have the honor of serving something greater than my self-interest."[2]

That was his conclusion as he graduated from the Naval Academy in 1958. His earlier life had hardly been a monument to a lack of self-interest. He was known as a nonconformist with a "defiant, unruly streak."[3] His nickname in high school was "Punk." His picture in his senior yearbook showed him in a trench coat, collar up and cigarette dangling from his lips. This at an Episcopal high school. He was combative, rambunctious, and raffish. Friends remembered that he dressed in blue jeans and wore shoes held together by tape. His manner changed little at the Naval Academy, where he accumulated so many demerits—most for attitude and rebellion—that he ranked only 894 out of 899 midshipmen.[4]

The defining experience of his life came in 1967, when he was shot down during his twenty-third bombing mission over North Vietnam. There followed five and a half years of hellish treatment as a prisoner of war. In ejecting from his plane, he had broken both arms and a leg, none of which ever healed correctly. Soon after his capture, he dropped to a skeletal weight, suffered the agonies of dysentery, and was forced into two years of solitary confinement. Then there were the beatings, sometimes three a week, which nearly shattered him mentally as well as physically. Still, he clung to the character of his fathers, to the Christian values of the Navy and his Episcopal Church. As the son of a famous admiral, he might have won early release. He refused—both to sign a confession of war crimes and to accept release until the men imprisoned before him were set free. The beatings increased, and his suffering deepened beyond comprehension. Despairing, he attempted suicide repeatedly. Each time, his captors intervened. In time, he signed a statement admitting to war crimes, an act he describes as dishonorable on his part to this day.

Still, his faith sustained him. He "prayed more often and more fervently than I ever had as a free man," he later recalled, and because his Episcopal training had graced him with the memorized confessions of Christendom—the Apostles' Creed, the Lord's Prayer—his senior officers made him chaplain to the other prisoners. He led prayers, read Scripture, and put together services, later remembering one particular Christmas service as being "more sacred to me than any service I had attended in the past, or any service I have attended since."[5]

> Because McCain's Episcopal training had graced him with the memorized confessions of Christendom—the Apostles' Creed, the Lord's Prayer—his senior officers made him chaplain to the other prisoners.

He even tried to share his faith with his interrogators. When a young Vietnamese officer asked, "What is Easter?" McCain withheld nothing: "I told him that it was the time of year we celebrated the death and resurrection of the Son of God. As I recounted the events of Christ's passion, His crucifixion, death, resurrection, and assumption to heaven, I saw my curious interrogator furrow his brow in disbelief."

"You say He died?"

"Yes, He died."

"Three days, He was dead?"

"Yes, then He came alive again. People saw Him, and then He went back to heaven."

Later, the interrogator, having asked another Vietnamese officer about McCain's faith, returned in anger. "Mac Kane, the officer say you tell nothing but lies. Go back to your room," he ordered, "the mystery of my faith proving incomprehensible to him," as McCain later concluded.[6]

During one particularly horrific season in camp, McCain found himself standing in an exercise yard on Christmas Day. A guard approached him, stood silently for a moment, and then drew a cross in the dirt with his foot. The two stared at the symbol wordlessly for several minutes before the guard simply walked away. Though McCain never had any other meaningful contact with the guard, he took those few moments before that dirt cross as a sign of God's grace. They may, too, have been evidence of his parents' prayers. He would return home to learn from his mother of how his father prayed for him on his knees in his study, of how she would hear him through the door, pleading, "God, show Johnny mercy."[7]

And mercy came. McCain was released in 1973, resumed his flying for the Navy in 1974, and served until 1981. In 1983, he successfully ran for Congress, launching the political career that twenty-five years later carried him to the Republican nomination for the presidency.

He conducted his political life under a cloud of religious suspicion, however. Typical of his generation—and of his father's generation before him—McCain was not comfortable speaking publicly about a personal matter like faith. He had been weaned in a culture that measured faith by deeds, that distrusted excessive religious talk but valued religion confirmed by good works and character. Silent character. Unpreachy character. Character that would never vaunt religion for political gain.

The press often grew frustrated. The details of McCain's faith were sketchy. Though an Episcopalian, McCain began attending North Phoenix Baptist Church when he married his second wife, Cindy. Ever the maverick, he never agreed to be baptized—the confirmation of true faith in a Baptist church—neither did he ever officially join the church. Then there was the famous outburst against Pat Robertson and Jerry Falwell. In an often-debated speech, he called them "agents of intolerance." Friends said he made the statement because he was angry at lies used against him in the hotly contested South Carolina primary of 2000, lies he believes Falwell and Robertson encouraged. The McCains had adopted a dark-skinned daughter whom they first met at Mother Teresa's orphanage in Bangladesh. Rumors circulated that McCain had immorally fathered a child with an African-American woman. This was a lie, of course, carefully crafted to appeal to the assumed racism of South Carolina. It was easy to understand how such a charge could enrage a man and send him on the attack.

His refusal to speak in detail about his faith reminds many of another man, one of an earlier but similar generation, who had difficulty in expressing spiritual truth with clarity: George H. W. Bush. He, too, is Episcopalian and of a culture that did not easily speak of personal religion. Once asked what he thought about while floating in the Sea of Japan after being shot down during World War II, the elder Bush said, "Mom and Dad, about our country, about God . . . and about the separation of church and state."[8] When asked by an increasingly powerful Religious Right about what gets a man into heaven, Bush would fumble and haltingly offer truisms about virtue, about being a good man and loving other people. No one was satisfied. McCain is of much the same culture, much the same generation, much the same sense of honor for the private and closely guarded matters of the heart.

Yet McCain seeks the presidency in a tell-all age, in an Obama-age of confession, of personal struggles dramatically portrayed in best-selling books, and of religious fluency. There will be a conflict of cultures. McCain will speak of a God whose blessing he seeks as he serves his country with honor. His opponent will likely speak in warm terms of a faith that fills the soul, of

> *McCain will look like George Washington praying at Valley Forge. His opponent will hold a press conference after buying a personalized Bible at the mall.*

a mission that springs from the beloved words of Scripture. McCain will speak of tried-and-true values and of the American way. His opponent will speak of the teachings of Jesus and of making America a more righteous land. McCain will say that he prays, goes to church, and reads his Bible, but then will say little more. His opponent will invite the press into Bible studies and distribute pages from spiritual journals written at transforming retreats. McCain will look like George Washington praying at Valley Forge. His opponent will hold a press conference after buying a personalized Bible at the mall.

This, then, is one face of American faith, one faith-based political vision vying for influence in the 2008 election. McCain represents this vision and those who hold it. They are the older, more traditional, less publicly religious tribe who fought their wars, endured cultural upheavals with almost stoic nobility, and realize that their generation may have only one more chance to hold the presidency, one more chance to embed the values of the founding and defending of America into a younger generation who have paid little for the freedoms they enjoy.

There is another face of American faith. It might be called the un-McCain. It belongs to those raised in the wake of World War II, those born in that explosion of life—now more than 80 million strong—often termed *the baby boom*. A generation of spiritual seekers, they are known both for their magnificent creativity and their debilitating instability, for their genius and their tortured flaws. And for those of this clan who cling to traditional religion but long for a politically liberal America, Hillary Clinton is the symbol of the dream.

The defining image of Hillary Clinton's early life came from her family's memory that great ancestors had been converted under John Wesley in the coal fields of England. It is an image that has burned itself into her mind. The penetrating sermon by the Oxford don. The coal dust–darkened faces streaked by tears. The gospel come to the poor. It is this distinctly Methodist merging of gospel and social conscience that has framed her sense of mission all her days.

She was born in 1947 to a Republican home in Chicago, to a father of deep faith—yet who seldom attended church—and was often compared to General George Patton, and to a mother who provided the nurturing center of her life and faith. "We talked with God," Hillary remembered later. "We walked with God, ate, studied and argued with God. Each night we knelt by our beds to pray."[9]

The vision of Methodism that captured her young heart is best summarized in Wesley's famous charge, "Do all the good you can, by all the means you can, in all the ways you can, at all the times you can, to all the people you can, as long as you ever can." She was mentored in these values by a recent Drew University graduate named Don Jones, who entered her life when she was just thirteen. As the new youth minister at her church, Jones decided to break from the sleepy ways of youth ministers past and thrust his charges into confrontation with the crises of the age. The civil rights movement was just then gaining momentum, racial tension was tearing at the nation's soul, and a gentle culture of youthful dissent was haltingly finding its voice. Jones intended to train those under his care to be relevant to it all. He taught of Jesus and John Wesley, yes, but also of existentialism, Beat poetry, folk music, and the Cultural Revolution. He once asked his youth group to meditate while Bob Dylan's "A Hard Rain's a-Gonna Fall" sounded in their ears. He often worked from poetry more than Scripture and showed art house films to stir discussion. He was fearless, inviting an atheist to debate the existence of God before his wide-eyed youth and leading a discussion of teen pregnancy that set the whole congregation abuzz.

Of lasting impact on Hillary's life, he forced his group to recognize social ills by taking them on field trips beyond their middle-class world. Once he merged his privileged white teens with youth from the inner city, and gathered them all around a print of Picasso's *Guernica*, a painting of the devastations of war. Discussion followed, with Hillary's friends speaking of war only in the most abstract terms. Then, after a silence, one inner-city girl quietly said, "Just last week, my uncle drove up and parked on the street and some guy came up to him and said you can't park there, that's my parking place, and my uncle resisted him and the guy pulled out a gun and shot him."[10] Jones's white youth group was stunned, Hillary in particular, and the experience gave rise to one of the most important experiences in all their lives: a trip to hear Martin Luther King Jr. speak at Chicago's Orchestra Hall in April 1962.

Perceiving that fifteen-year-old Hillary had a keen mind and a potentially keen social conscience, Jones began to mentor her in his worldview. He urged her to read Tillich, Niebuhr, Kierkegaard, and Bonheoffer, and met with her as she did to discuss her reflections. He thought nothing of assigning both J. D. Salinger's *Catcher in the Rye* and a Methodist devotional, Beat author Jack Kerouac and the Bible. Jones wanted Hillary to understand that the heart of Christianity is social duty, that faith relieves the suffering of others, or it is dead.

She became his willing convert and carried the social gospel of her Methodism through Wellesley, Yale Law School, and marriage to the Baptist Bill Clinton. There followed the storied rise through Arkansas politics and then the White House in 1992. Throughout these years, though Hillary strove to live the social calling of her faith, she was plagued by a crisis of perception, by the unceasing charges that she actually "had no religion" and that she was, in truth, "a godless liberal."[11] Such charges were troubling to her and to those who knew her well. She was a woman of prayer and Bible study who could quote Wesley at length and speak warmly and comfortably of God's work in her life. Yet the suspicion persisted that her religion was a facade, that she faked faith for political gain.

During seasons when these charges reached high tide, Hillary tried to explain herself as clearly as she could. In 1994, for example, she was interviewed by Kenneth Woodward of *Newsweek*. Claiming that "the Clintons are perhaps the most openly religious first couple this century has seen," Woodward explored Hillary's statement that she is an "old-fashioned Methodist" by subjecting her to the kind of detailed grilling usually reserved for new converts.

Woodward: "Do you believe in the Father, Son and Holy Spirit?"
First Lady: "Yes"
Woodward: "The atoning death of Jesus?"
First Lady: "Yes."
Woodward: "The resurrection of Christ?"
First Lady: "Yes."[12]

Hillary also commented on the direction of her church. Telling Woodward that she kept a copy of *The Book of Resolutions of the United Methodist Church* beside her Bible—a claim that drew snickers from the press—she added, "I think that the Methodist Church, for a period of time, became too socially concerned, too involved in the social gospel, and did not pay enough attention to questions of personal salvation and individual faith."[13] This was surprising coming from Don Jones's disciple, from a woman drawn to Methodism more by its social vision than by matters of the spirit, but it may have signaled a new emphasis in her faith. In the interview, she also described reading Christian authors such as Henri Nouwen, Gordon MacDonald, and Tony Campolo. Though Campolo's writings focus on social justice, Nouwen and MacDonald speak more of the inner life, of the healing of the heart from the wounds and temptations of this world. Naturally, critics saw nothing in the interview but a politician making the required nods to faith, but Hillary's emphasis on the personal and the interior may have signaled much about the state of her soul.

The truth is that Hillary had long endured a series of the most soul-crushing experiences a woman can know: the marital unfaithfulness of her husband. Insiders knew that Bill Clinton was a man of nearly unchecked appetites and that his sexual passion was no exception. He bedded women with frequency, enlisted staff in cover-ups, and betrayed Hillary even with her friends. His behavior sliced deeply into her heart. As always with Bill, there were tearful confessions and promises to stop. Divorce would be discussed, but always there was pleading and a counselor urging devotion to the marriage. Still, the agony of it all thrust Hillary upon the comforts of her God, deepening her faith and her desperation for a greater spiritual reality.

This desperation moved religion to the forefront of both her personal and her public life. She attended women's prayer meetings, invited religious leaders to dinner at the White House, and devoured books on experientially knowing God. She also stayed in touch with Don Jones, then a professor of social ethics at Drew University, and tried to bring her faith to play in her politics as he had taught her to do. She was clumsy in her efforts and often disturbingly vague, speaking of a "politics of meaning" and of using "God-given gifts" to heal society. Her attempts at connecting the spiritual to the political seemed to her critics like pious mush, yet little she could have said would have won them. The dominant religious voices in American politics at the time were from the Right, and if you weren't "born again" and you weren't conservative in your politics, then you were just an insincere religious echo from the Left.

It didn't help that Hillary ventured far afield from her Methodist moorings into what many considered to be the occult. She had long felt a kinship with Eleanor Roosevelt, who, like her, endured an unfaithful husband, a Republican barrage, and the bruisings that come to a gifted woman in an unwelcoming age. Hillary mentioned Mrs. Roosevelt often in her speeches and even described imaginary conversations that left her feeling strong and inspired. One of the New Age leaders who had been welcomed at the

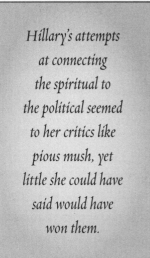

Hillary's attempts at connecting the spiritual to the political seemed to her critics like pious mush, yet little she could have said would have won them.

White House, Jean Houston, suggested that Hillary "search further and deeper" into her connection with FDR's departed wife. According to Bob Woodward's account in *The Choice*, Houston arranged a session in the White House solarium, in which she encouraged Hillary to conjure an image of Eleanor Roosevelt and then open her heart.

Hillary addressed Eleanor, focusing on her predecessor's fierceness and determination, her advocacy on behalf of people in need. Hillary continued to address Eleanor, discussing the obstacles, the criticism, the loneliness the former First Lady felt. Her identification with Mrs. Roosevelt was intense and personal. They were members of an exclusive club of women who could comprehend the complexity, the ambiguity of their position. It's hard, Hillary said. Why was there such a need in people to put other people down? . . . I was misunderstood, Hillary replied, her eyes still shut, speaking as Mrs. Roosevelt. You have to do what you think is right, she continued. It was crucial to set a course and hold it.[14]

The contact with Roosevelt made, Houston then tried to facilitate conversations with Mahatma Gandhi and even Jesus Christ, according to Woodward. Hillary balked at the idea of talking to the Son of God in this way, though, and brought the session to an end.

When the tales of what amounted to a séance reached the public, Hillary was humiliated. Critics guffawed, the Religious Right charged demonic activity, and the general public looked with disgust on the antics of a self-absorbed First Lady who had become spiritually unhinged. Hillary tried to answer: "The bottom line is, I have no spiritual advisors or any other alternatives to my deeply held Methodist faith and traditions on which I have relied since childhood."[15] Trying to lighten the mood, she reported in a speech, "I have just had an imaginary talk with First Lady Roosevelt, and she thinks this is a terrific idea."[16] Such joking helped damage control but did not calm the storm of opposition against her. What many had not noticed in the riot of opinionated response to the session with Houston was the desperation of a wounded woman and her obviously unmet spiritual longings.

The Hillary Clinton of the séance was religiously the only Hillary most Americans would know until years later when she was elected to the U.S. Senate from New York. This came about in

2000, just as George W. Bush was ascending to the presidency in a campaign that had been as much about faith as any in history to that time. There was, as a result, a more religiously open culture in Washington, and it was only broadened by spiritual passions poured out following the terrors of September 11, 2001. Hillary took much of this renewed spiritual openness as her own, and Americans soon met a different woman than they had known before, one who seemed at ease with God and her faith as a framing for her political role. She conversed casually about the writings of Thomas Aquinas and Saint Augustine, spoke of feeling "the presence of the Holy Spirit on many occasions" and filled her speeches with scripture and references to prayer.[17]

In her Senate years, Hillary seemed a woman more whole than she had been, but no less hungry for spiritual truth. She was a regular at Capitol prayer meetings, and even showed up at religious events planned by Republican Majority Leader Tom DeLay, the man who had led the charge to impeach her husband. She also attended conferences such as those sponsored by Sojourners, the progressive Christian organization that urged the priority of social justice in the service of God. Friends reported too that her political and personal sufferings had dug a deep well in her life and that she now yearned to draw from that well to inspire the nation as a whole.

This, then, is the Hillary Clinton who has run for office in 2008. She was born in a *Father Knows Best* age but was introduced earlier than most to the roiling unrest hidden beneath the surface of a comfortable, self-satisfied America. Exceptionally bright and gifted, not unlike many of her generation, she rose quickly through savvy and education, although she sustained lasting wounds in the culture wars of her public life, in the humiliations of her own excesses, and in the private agonies of a husband's betrayal. Still, she clung to the defining vision of her life: the Methodist charge to serve others as widely as possible to the glory of God.

Her opponent, though, is not so inspired by her story of faith. Barack Obama has written that the bitter partisanship of the 2000 and 2004 elections—Hillary's era in the Senate—reflected "the psychodrama of the baby boom generation—a tale rooted in the old grudges and revenge plots hatched on a handful of college campuses long ago."[18] He does not see in Hillary's tribe grizzled veterans of the Cultural Revolution. He sees them instead as many see Hillary herself: a self-absorbed, scheming, self-pitying bunch who feel themselves entitled to every freedom, all while building monuments in the souls of their children to their own addictions and irresponsibilities. Obama's Millennials resent Hillary's Boomers for their narcissistic individuality, for thinking that life is about them and them alone. Indeed, Obama likely longs for political power, in part, to fix what Hillary's generation has left broken and unfulfilled in the American dream.

Obama likely longs for political power, in part, to fix what Hillary's generation has left broken and unfulfilled in the American dream.

Nevertheless, Hillary is another face of the American spirituality come to contend in the nation's public square. It is the face of those who said, "No more" to their parents' comfortable 1950s conformity and so have proceeded to remake the nation and set it on a journey of a different kind. It is the face of those who cling to traditional faith but unceasingly rework that faith into a more modern form. It is the face of those who find in the ethics of Jesus a mandate for the welfare state. And it is the face of those who trust others like them, and so find in Hillary a leader who is wounded and wearied but undeterred in the quest to make America fulfill her democratic promise.

The third face of American political religion is one familiar but fading from the current public square. It is the face of those who looked out over the landscape of Hillary Clinton's 1960s and found their version of America going away. In the sexual revolution, in the widest possible separation of religion and state, and later in the legalization of abortion, they found a mandate to reclaim what had been lost, to call America to faith once again. These were the evangelicals, the awakened Moral Majority, those eager to connect the nation to her moorings in holy passion and to her call to be a "City upon a Hill." This is the face of George W. Bush.

Some will question why his story should be considered at all. Isn't his a story of the past? Hasn't he led the country in a direction many wish to correct? Isn't it time to put his story to an end? Perhaps so, but before we do, we must recall that it was George W. Bush's openness about his beliefs that first helped to make faith an acceptable part of the political landscape in America. It was Bush whose evangelical conversion story has defined his presidency— perhaps *the* presidency—in unmistakable ways. And it is Bush's tale of faith against which all other presidential journeys of faith will be compared for decades to come. Yes, his story, too, is one of the defining tales of faith in contemporary American politics.

Bush was born in 1946 to a war hero father and to a plain-spoken mother descended from President Franklin Pierce. He, like Hillary Clinton, would be a baby boomer, yet with a Texas, upper-class twist.

Though his family had been New Englanders for generations, Bush grew up in West Texas—in a world of cattle and oil, of gun racks on pickup trucks, rattlesnake roundups, and tumbleweeds so plentiful that some West Texans painted them for Christmas. His early life was steeped in religion, but of a formal and distant kind. He was baptized in an Episcopal church in New Haven, Connecticut, where he was born. His family then attended the First Presbyterian Church of Midland, Texas, after George's father moved west to test his fate in oil. Ten years later, after a move to Houston, the family worshipped at St. Martin's Episcopal Church, where Bush said he first felt "stirrings of faith."[19] Then there were years at Phillips Academy Andover, where five times a week he attended a Congregationalist-style chapel. By the time he went to Yale in 1964, he began taking religion in small doses. Perhaps he needed a break.

The besetting disease of Bush after Yale was an agonizing aimless-ness, an absence of any sense of destiny. It crippled him and kept him from his best. A friend from this time recalls, "I don't think he'd figured out what he liked about himself yet, or what he liked about life, except for baseball."[20] It didn't change after college. He became a Houston playboy, driving a Triumph, dating beautiful women—including the daughter of designer Oleg Cassini—and learning to fly jets for the Texas Air National Guard at nearby Ellington Air Force Base. He was living a shallow life. He had a trickle of Christianity running through his soul, but it was far from a controlling current.

There followed an MBA at Harvard, marriage to Laura, and unsuccessful years in the West Texas oil fields. There was even an unwise and lackluster run for Congress. Nothing brought success. He settled but did not know who he was. He also began to drink—and drink heavily. To this day, friends in Midland/Odessa remember him as the drunk at the end of the bar who thought himself more hilarious the more whiskey he drank.

Foolishly, and after a night of drinking with his brother, he once challenged his father to a fight. There may have been more in this than loss of self-control. As his cousin John Ellis has said, Bush was "on the road to nowhere at forty." It was a crisis of comparison, he believes:

> You have to really understand how much his father was loved and respected by so many people to understand what it would be like to grow up as a namesake, the son of George Bush. These are the parallels in his life. He went to Andover, went to Yale, went to West Texas, ran for Congress, and at every stage of that he was found wanting. To go through every stage of life and be found wanting and know that people find you wanting, that's a real grind.[21]

The change began during an area-wide revival service held in Midland/Odessa, conducted by evangelist Arthur Blessitt. Bush avoided the emotionalism of the meetings, with their fiery altar calls and tearful converts, but asked for a private meeting with

Blessitt. The evangelist agreed, and the two met along with some friends in April 1984.

"Arthur," Bush began, "I did not feel comfortable attending the meeting, but I want to talk to you about how to know Jesus Christ and how to follow Him."[22]

The evangelist reflected for a moment and asked, "What is your relationship with Jesus?"

"I'm not sure," Bush replied.

"Let me ask you this question," Blessitt probed. "If you died this moment, do you have the assurance you would go to heaven?"

Bush did not hesitate. "No," he answered.

Blessitt shared some scriptures and then said, "The call of Jesus is for us to repent and believe. The choice is like this. Would you rather live with Jesus in your life or live without Him?"

"With Him," Bush replied.

Then, after more words of instruction, Blessitt said, "Mr. Bush, I would like to pray a prayer for you and then lead you in a prayer of commitment and salvation. You can become a follower of Jesus now."

"I'd like that," Bush said. And so the preacher and the vice president's son bowed in prayer.

It was a beginning, yet the final turning would come the next year, during days spent with Billy Graham at the Bush home in Kennebunkport. Barbara Bush had sensed her son's spiritual hunger and invited Graham to join the family gathering in hopes that he might help George find his way to God. One evening, Graham spoke to the family and, as Bush later recalled, "It was this beautiful Maine night and Billy just sat there and talked to us and we asked him questions and shared our thoughts. He and I had a visit after-ward—it was just a real personal religious visit—and I started reading the Bible."[23] The "visit afterward" was a walk that Graham and Bush took at Walker's Point the next day. During the conversa-tion, Graham turned to Bush and said, "Are you right with God?"

"No," Bush replied, "but I want to be."[24] The two spent more hours together over the following days. As Bush later wrote of that time:

> Reverend Graham planted a mustard seed in my soul, a seed that grew over the next year. I had always been a religious person, had regularly attended church, even taught Sunday school and served as an altar boy. But that weekend my faith took on new meaning. It was the beginning of a new walk where I would recommit my heart to Jesus Christ. I was humbled to learn that God sent His Son to die for a sinner like me.[25]

Unlike many who are converted and then are left to make their own way, Bush immediately joined a men's Community Bible Study (CBS) in Midland. This was part of a nationwide movement of nondenominational Bible studies that focused on the story of Scripture, on the meaning for an individual's life apart from the traditional overlay of sectarian dogma. Bush thrived in this approach. Friends soon noticed that he tamed his foul language, and then, to the amazement of all, he stopped drinking. These were the first steps of self-mastery, of showing himself capable of finding the discipline to serve a greater cause. Years later, when he had ascended to the presidency, he asked some religious leaders to pray for him by saying, "You know, I had a drinking problem. Right now I should be in a bar in Texas, not the Oval Office. There is only one reason that I am in the Oval Office and not in a bar. I found faith. I found God. I am here because of the power of prayer."[26]

> *"You know, I had a drinking problem. Right now I should be in a bar in Texas, not the Oval Office. There is only one reason that I am in the Oval Office and not in a bar. I found faith. I found God. I am here because of the power of prayer."*

The years that followed his conversion were more of a swirl than those who loved him might have wished, given his need to steep in his newfound evangelical Christianity. He soon after became an advisor to his father's presidential campaign and then, having left the oil business, became an owner of the Texas Rangers. The role gave him fame throughout Texas, which he parlayed into a successful campaign for governor, defeating the widely popular Ann Richards in an astonishing upset. His years in the governor's mansion let him test some of his beliefs—in a new brand of faith-based social action and in a partnership between government and the private sector to accomplish social good.

During these years, another vision formed in Bush's mind: to run for the presidency. His most revealing discussion of his thinking at the time came in a conversation with evangelist James Robison, who had been instrumental in encouraging Ronald Reagan to run for president in 1980.

"My life is changed," the governor said. "I had a drinking problem. I won't say I was an alcoholic, but it affected my relationships, even with my kids. It could have destroyed me. But I've given my life to Christ."[27]

Robison, who had heard rumors of Bush's conversion, was struck by the sincerity he sensed. He was not prepared, though, for what came next.

"I feel like God wants me to run for president," Bush said. "I can't explain it, but I sense my country is going to need me. Something is going to happen and, at that time, my country is going to need me. I know it won't be easy, on me or my family, but God wants me to do it. In fact, I really don't want to run. My father was president. My whole family has been affected by it. I know the price. I know what it will mean. I would be perfectly happy to have people point at me someday when I'm buying my fishing lures at Wal-Mart and say, 'That was our governor.' That's all I want. And if I run for president, that kind of life will be over. My life will never be the same. But I know God wants me to do this and I must do it."[28]

And so he ran. It would be one of the most unusual presidential races on record, ultimately decided by one of the most controversial Supreme Court decisions in history. But Bush would win. Twice. During his years in office, he would face some of the most challenging crises any president had known: September 11, 2001, and the invasions of Afghanistan and Iraq, Hurricane Katrina, and a global economy in tumult. Sadly, none of it ended well during his time in office.

To the extent that his presidency was a proving ground for innovative policies—faith-based initiatives, a doctrine of preemptive military action, a neoconservative faith in America as the guarantor of global democracy—his administration's missteps wrapped those policies in an aura of failure. His years in office were perhaps best summarized by journalist and professor Marvin Olasky, once Bush's mentor on faith-based social policy, when he said that the Bush team reinvented politics but failed to reinvent governance. It was true. In the end, there was no galvanizing vision, no rallying dream to pull the nation through.

For Obama, Bush is the face of the Religious Right, a movement that used faith to divide and conquer while in pursuit of political power, and then didn't know what to do with that power once they had it in hand. As he told a convention of his own United Church of Christ denomination in 2007:

Somehow, somewhere along the way, faith stopped being used to bring us together and started being used to drive us apart. It got hijacked . . . Part of it's because of the so-called leaders of the Christian Right, who've been all too eager to exploit what divides us . . . At every opportunity, they've told evangelical Christians that Democrats disrespect their values and dislike their church, while suggesting to the rest of the country that religious Americans care only about issues like abortion and gay marriage; school prayer and intelligent design . . . There was even a time when the Christian Coalition determined that its number one legislative priority was tax cuts for the rich . . . I don't know what Bible they're reading, but it doesn't jibe with my version.[29]

FOUR FACES OF FAITH

This, then, is what many Americans hear as Obama's critique of Bush: *You rose on the strength of a vicious use of faith. You then baptized a greedy conservative agenda and called its God's will. Along the way, you labeled us Democrats as somehow antifaith. Now, your political faith failing you, your religious base abandoning you, it is time for you to go away. A new faith, based in the genuine compassion of the Religious Left, is waiting in the wings. Step aside, and let us heal what you have broken.*

And so George W. Bush, champion of the Religious Right and of baby boomers gone conservative, stands beside the other stories of faith shaping the politics of 2008. Beside John McCain, stalwart of the faith of the fathers, of the God and country heritage, of religion as a private and holy concern. Beside Hillary Clinton, whose Methodism moves her to seek a new Great Society, whose wounds and failures only win her devotion from a generation who has known the same but who live on to seek the America of the Cultural Revolution's dreams.

And then there is Obama. His face stands out among them all. It is black. It is under fifty in 2008. It is Christian in a nontraditional sense. It is Columbia and Harvard. It is progressive and social justice and the most liberal face of all. And his face, all the signs suggest, is the face of the future. Whether he wins the race in 2008 or not, Obama is what America is becoming. So he takes his place among the four faces of faith, and he publicly welcomes a chance to stand on the stage with McCain and Clinton and Bush. But the others are the faces of warriors past. He alone, he believes, carries the future.

6

A Time to Heal

It is the healers who are best remembered, those who teach us to live beyond the limitations of our lesser selves. The healers are greathearts and lovers—souls who show us the path to the world we've hoped for, who teach us that we can make our high-flying rhetoric into living, earthly reality.

They tend to come after bruising, bloody seasons, and yet they seem immune to the rage and vengeance of lesser men. They know how to grasp forgiveness and generosity of heart, having usually mined these traits from the dark valleys of their own lives. Thankfully, they rise to grace a public stage and then heal their land and their people with the truths hard-won in less-visible days. Nations, then, are unified. Political strife is transformed into statesmanship. Races are ennobled and readied to belong to a broader whole. Men and women are freed from the grip of the petty and the small. This is what healers do.

Abraham Lincoln comes to mind. From the depths of a life haunted by the deepest emotional depression, he wrung a generosity of soul that resisted the fierce hatreds of his time. He appointed his political rivals as members of his cabinet, pleaded for forgiveness as the Civil War drew to an end, and called his nation to greatness in grand sentences that live on: "With malice toward none; with charity for all; with firmness in the right, as God gives us to see the right, let us strive on to finish the work we are in; to bind up the nation's wounds; to care for him who shall have borne the battle, and for his widow, and his orphan—to do all which may achieve and cherish a just and lasting peace, among ourselves, and with all nations."[1]

Abraham Lincoln was a healer. Nelson Mandela was too. Though imprisoned for terrorism against a racist state, Mandela emerged decades later to lead in the healing of his land. "If there are dreams about a beautiful South Africa," he once said, "there are also roads that lead to their goal. Two of these roads could be named Goodness and Forgiveness."

There is, of course, Martin Luther King Jr., who might have stood on the steps of the Lincoln Memorial in 1963 and vented the rage of his people. Instead, he urged a faith that would "transform the jangling discords of our nation into a beautiful symphony of brotherhood." He was a healer.

And some healers heal by deed if not by word. Only at the funeral of former president Gerald Ford did we come to understand what we should have known long before: that Ford was a man of exceptional goodness who "drew out the poisons released by Vietnam and Watergate."[2] He did not live in an age as epic as Lincoln's; neither did he possess King's rhetorical gifts, but he was a healer by character and condition of soul, and at a time when his nation needed him but did not understand the sign of grace that he was.

There are others, of course: the Gandhis and the Washingtons, men like Desmond Tutu and William Wilberforce, women like Benazir Bhutto and Golda Meir. They will all be well remembered, for warriors are remembered with awe and statesmen with respect, but it is the healers who are remembered with love.

It was William Shakespeare who wrote in *Julius Caesar*:

> There is a tide in the affairs of men,
> Which taken at the flood, leads on to fortune;
> Omitted, all the voyage of their life
> Is bound in shallows and in miseries.
> On such a full sea are we now afloat;
> And we must take the current when it serves,
> Or lose our ventures."[3]

Shakespeare's character Brutus seems to be saying that fate sometimes offers opportunity that must be recognized and then embraced. To do so leads to glory. To fail to recognize the destined moment is to remain in the shallows, in the immobility of low tide, in the miserable contemplation of what might have been.

The American people find themselves in just such a situation.

There is before them an opportunity that may, if they choose, be embraced as the path to a new history. It is an opportunity to heal, to take the historic wounds and generational conflicts that political debates are shoving to the fore and respond to them in the spirit of the great healers, in the manner of those who wish to fashion a future rather a short-term political victory.

Yet this new history is not likely to be fashioned by politics and by the doings of government. Far from it. We should remember the words of columnist George Will, who wrote, "There is hardly a page of American history that does not refute that insistence, so characteristic of the political class, on the primacy of politics in the making of history."[4] Therefore, Will contends, "Almost nothing is as important as almost everything in Washington is made to appear. And the importance of a Washington event is apt to be inversely proportional to the attention it receives."[5] And this is as the founding generation expected it to be, for as Patrick Henry stated, "Liberty necessitates the diminutization of political ambition and concern. Liberty necessitates concentration on other matters than mere civil governance."[6] No, government is not likely to create the new history now offered to our generation. Oddly, though, it is politics that is pushing onto the national stage the issues that, rightly treated, may lead to that new history.

The 2008 election season is a historic time. Seldom in American history has religion been so much at the forefront of a presidential election. Rarely have different generations been so starkly represented. Never has a black man or a woman advanced so far. And never has technology been as capable of carrying each word and deed as instantaneously to a watching world. Yet the 2008 election season is also a historic time because of the airing of national wounds and sins that is taking place on a virtually unprecedented scale. Indeed, it may well prove that this is the longer-term importance of this thrashing time in our history, just as it may well prove that this is the more important meaning of Barack Obama's presence in our history at this moment.

Shelby Steele has made the case in his *A Bound Man: Why We Are Excited About Obama and Why He Can't Win* that Obama is more significant for *who* he is than for *what* he does politically. Whether or not

> Whether or not he wins his party's nomination and the presidency, Obama is meaningful to our time for what he represents.

he wins his party's nomination and the presidency, Obama is meaningful to our time for what he represents that is therefore placed under the national spotlight: The challenges of the biracial person. The cause of the poor. The rise of a new generation. The restoration of religion to the political Left. The manner, power, and moral case of the black church in America. Each of these Obama brings with him to the public debate, to his struggle for the presidency, and this then gives our age the possibility of responding beyond politics and party strife to the grievances of some in our extended American family.

Let us take race as an example. Nothing has beset the Obama candidacy like the presence of the Reverend Jeremiah A. Wright Jr. before the national gaze. Once Americans heard snippets of Wright's sermons and caught his manner before the press, they concluded that he was a madman, a nut, a racist, an older black man hopefully passing with all those like him from the scene. Politics demanded that Obama distance himself from the man—his pastor, his mentor, his friend—and so he did, claiming, as some termed it, "the crazy old uncle defense": that Wright had once been brilliant and gifted but now was descending into the foolishness all can see. It was painful to watch, and most Americans will simply regard it as an oddity in yet another cycle of crazy in American politics.

Could it be, though, that what has happened offers the nation an opportunity, a strategic moment, for healing and grace? Is it possible that, beyond the politics of the moment and even the larger presidential race, there is Shakespeare's tide to be taken at the flood, an open door of healing for the land?

Jeremiah Wright is not crazy. He is an educated man with four earned degrees, respected in his church and his denomination, who has been an honored voice of black America. When the Clinton administration sought to cleanse both itself and the nation of the Lewinsky scandal, Wright was among those invited to the White House. When black churches nationwide yearn to experience spiritual revival, they often call Jeremiah Wright. When leading seminaries wish to understand black religious thought, they call, among others, Jeremiah Wright. Despite his often unusual behavior before the national press—surely the antics of a hurt and angry man—all the evidence indicates that this is a man in his right mind, articulating a message shared by millions. To claim him crazy and dismiss him from the scene without a hearing is to miss an opportunity to heal a grievous, festering wound.

What Wright contends is that the United States government is more often a force of oppression than of good. He argues that there are national sins that must be addressed, wrongs inflicted by our government on the helpless at home and abroad that displease God and—if the biblical law of sowing and reaping is true—may bring ill on Americans at home; their "chickens coming home to roost." So rigorous is he in exposing these wrongs, so committed to resisting the oppressor in aid of the oppressed, that he told Obama—his friend, his parishioner—in 2007, "If you get elected, November the fifth, I'm coming after you, because you'll be representing a government whose policies grind under people."[7]

And what are these national wrongs? There is slavery, of course, and the ill treatment of Native Americans. There is also the charge of police oppression in America's inner cities. These are not unexpected. Yet Wright goes further. He charges that his government commits acts of medical abuse on blacks. He believes that people of color are sacrificed in immoral wars abroad and that those very wars spread misery and murder throughout the world. He argues that even our most revered presidents lied to their fellow citizens, and that time and again, wickedness more than righteousness infuses American foreign policy. And he is not alone. These sentiments sound from black pulpits throughout the country, as well as from the scholars and writers who share their cause.

We should pause to reflect that if half of these charges are true, they ought to be the concern of more than just black ministers. Any citizen who takes American values to heart should be both astonished and ashamed. Any faith that values compassion and holds human life as made in a divine image should be appalled and seek to make amends. Perhaps, if even part of Wright's charges are true, his claims during the 2008 campaign season present an opportunity to heal historic wounds. Perhaps this is a call for all of us to be more Christian than Republican, more American than Democrat, more noble and righteous than crassly and callously political. Perhaps, too, this is an opportunity to hear truth from the mouths of our critics.

For the fact is that some of what Wright says is true and more than the matters of slavery and native peoples and police behavior, all of which are well-known. The fact is that the American government has in the past engaged in medical abuse of blacks. Wright's suspicions that his government may not have his race's best interest at heart are not fantasy, and the compassionate in American society should try to understand why.

From 1932 until 1972, more than four hundred black men with syphilis from Macon County, Alabama, were enrolled in a medical study in which treatment for their affliction was denied. Called the Tuskegee Syphilis Study, the program was operated by the U.S. Public Health Service. In the study, men with syphilis were not told of their true disease, but were informed that they were being treated for *bad blood*, a local term used to describe a variety of illnesses, such as anemia and fatigue. Even after 1947, when penicillin became the standard cure for syphilis, the antibiotic was withheld so that researchers could study how syphilis spreads and kills. As a result, dozens of men died, wives and children were infected, and the study continued until 1972, when public health workers leaked the story to the press. The next year, in 1973, a class-action lawsuit led to a $9 million settlement that was shared by the remaining participants. [8]

The lesson was not lost on Jeremiah Wright's generation, though other abuses had already driven the message home: our government will allow black men to die as guinea pigs for medical research. This message embedded in the hearts of black Americans just as Wright took the lead of Trinity United Church of Christ, just as black theology was beginning to shape the African-American church.

Twenty-four years after the experiment ended, President Bill Clinton apologized for what his government had done. Saying that the Tuskegee Syphilis Study was "deeply, profoundly, morally wrong," Clinton concluded:

> To the survivors, to the wives and family members, the children and the grandchildren, I say what you know: No power on Earth can give you back the lives lost, the pain suffered, the years of internal torment and anguish. What was done cannot be undone. But we can end the silence. We can stop turning our heads away. We can look at you in the eye and finally say, on behalf of the American people: what the United States government did was shameful. And I am sorry.[9]

The meaning here is not that everything Rev. Wright contends is true, but that there is enough truth for a compassionate people to examine and treat redemptively. Surely, it is appropriate for the lies of government to be addressed, for example, much as Clinton addressed the immorality of the Tuskegee Study. Wright has suggested that Franklin Roosevelt knew in advance about the Japanese attack on Pearl Harbor, but lied to the American people. Commentators across the political spectrum, from Fox to CNN, guffawed in derision. Yet this view has long been discussed among serious academics, at least since Charles A. Beard wrote his *President Roosevelt and the Coming of the War, 1941* in 1948. It is not a view widely shared by modern historians, but it is academically credible enough to make us hesitate in dismissing Wright as a fool. Instead, his views ought to be heard, understood as those of a people within America, and addressed in an effort to heal.

Still, what offends many Americans is that Wright sounds his complaints from a Christian pulpit. Here there is a misunderstanding of the black church experience. From the days of slavery until now, the black church in America has seldom been just a Sunday morning meeting. It has been, in the earliest days, the few hours on a Sunday morning that slaves could call their own; to worship, yes, but also to hear the latest news, to plan for the good of the community, and to insulate as a people against the times. Later, when laws allowed, the black church became a prophetic voice against injustice, taking as its mission both to save individuals and to confront society with the will of the living God. This prophetic tradition, this addressing of both the spiritual and the societal, was what moved the black church to the forefront of the battle for civil rights and gave rise to men like Martin Luther King Jr. Consider, for example, King's understanding of the role between the church and the state:

> The church must be reminded that it is not the master or the servant of the state, but rather the conscience of the state. It must be the guide and the critic of the state, and never its tool. If the church does not recapture its prophetic zeal, it will become an irrelevant social club without moral or spiritual authority. If the

church does not participate actively in the struggle for peace and for economic and racial justice, it will forfeit the loyalty of millions and cause men everywhere to say that it has atrophied its will. But if the church will free itself from the shackles of a deadening status quo, and, recovering its great historic mission, will speak and act fearlessly and insistently in terms of justice and peace, it will enkindle the imagination of mankind and fire the souls of men, imbuing them with a glowing and ardent love for truth, justice, and peace.[10]

This is indicative of the tradition out of which Jeremiah Wright speaks, and a society as great as America believes herself to be ought to be able to hear him. When he suggests that poverty is at the same rate as when Martin Luther King Jr. launched his Poor People's Campaign in 1968, it is a point a great people ought to consider. When he argues that the sufferings of Native Americans should be addressed with more than the proceeds from gambling casinos, a righteous people ought to hear. And when his parishioner, Barack Obama, claims that "the path to a more perfect union means acknowledging that what ails the African American community does not just exist in the minds of black people; that the legacy of discrimination—and current incidents of discrimination, while less overt than in the past—are real and must be addressed,"[11] a people intending to be a great society must try to understand and act.

Yet this is how the story—and the hoped-for healing it portends—continues: with a new generation. In his "More Perfect Union" speech, in which he explained his history with Jeremiah Wright, Obama described himself in generational terms. Wright was

> Obama proclaimed himself a member of a new generation, a younger people committed to "embracing the burdens of our past without becoming the victims of our past."

of an age of blacks, he said, for whom "the memories of humiliation and doubt and fear have not gone away, nor has the anger and the bitterness of those years."[12] Obama proclaimed himself a member of a new generation, a younger people committed to "embracing the burdens of our past without becoming the victims of our past."[13] A change had come, he offered, and a new generation of African-Americans was now taking the reins.

This generational handoff is best symbolized by Rev. Wright's replacement at Trinity Church, Rev. Otis Moss. Though he is half Wright's age, he can speak movingly of family members lynched by a white mob in a Jim Crow South. Yet he does not share the rage, the debilitating bitterness, of those who have come before. Instead, like Obama, he has the task of a new generation, shaped by different forces, intent upon, perhaps, a loftier goal. "We are seeing on the political landscape people who are rising to the forefront who were very small during the civil rights movement or just not born at all," Moss has said. "But they don't lead by rejecting. They lead by bringing the past with them and bringing their own personal experiences."[14] This is what Moss celebrates in Obama's speech on race: "I also thought it was very good for him to share with the wider world the issues that an invisible America is facing and put these issues in the lap not only of this generation but the previous generation and say we have the ability to continue to build this cathedral of an unfinished democracy."[15]

It is in this unfinished democracy that Obama now finds his greatest challenge. He may well ascend to the presidency in time, and he may well craft a faith-based national agenda of his own. For now, he is giving a new generation a chance to address—in the calm of distance—what earlier generations endured in pain. He is pushing onto the national stage, merely by his presence, matters of poverty, race, religion, and age that the nation must address to ever be whole. He is granting America, then—whether he means to or not—an opportunity to heal.

While the nation ponders this open door of healing, though, Obama's faith is already helping to change both his party and many of the issues in the broader national debate. The 2008 campaign season—with its faith forums, the passions stirred by Jeremiah Wright, and a Democratic primary race between two vocal Christians—has been among the most religiously influenced of any in American history. Obama has held his own through it all, giving Americans opportunity to know details of his prayer life, his history in church, his relationship with his pastor, his theology of politics, and his views on a wide range of subjects, such as evolution and how best to interpret the Bible. In short, what Americans learned of George W. Bush's faith over a period of years has been revealed about Barack Obama during a single campaign season.

The change this represents in the Democratic Party is best understood from the journey of Howard Dean, now chairman of

THE FAITH OF BARACK OBAMA

> *Many Americans suspected Dean held religion in low regard when they learned that he had "left his Episcopal church over an argument concerning the placement of a bike path."*

the Democratic National Committee. When Dean ran for the presidency in 2003, he told his staff to avoid issues such as "guns, God and gays" and once boasted "my religion doesn't inform my public policy."[16] Many Americans suspected Dean held religion in low regard when they learned that he had "left his Episcopal church over an argument concerning the place-ment of a bike path."[17] As Mary Vanderslice, Dean's director of reli-gious outreach, concluded, in that 2003 campaign, evangelicals were "a target, not a target audi-ence."[18]

Now Dean presides over a party that some have called "The Church of the Religious Left." He schedules local faith forums, devises strategies to win the evangelical voters who are newly in play, and referees a contest between two primary candidates which is as much about faith as any other issue. His world has changed, and he has embraced it. Howard Dean, astute as few other politicians are, understands that he now functions in a political universe framed by religious worldviews. Though he accepts this, it often forces him against his natural grain. During an appearance on Pat Robertson's *700 Club*, Dean cheerily offered that Democrats "have an enormous amount in common with the Christian community."[19] Christians in the Democratic Party just shook their heads. Dean spoke as though there were no Democrats who were Christians, as though he were appealing to a people from another planet. Old ways are hard to unlearn.

Yet Dean will learn, and one of his teachers is certain to be Barack Obama. For Obama, faith is not simply political garb, something a focus group told him he ought to try. Instead, religion to him is transforming, lifelong, and real. It is who he is at the core, what he has raised his daughters to live, and the well he will draw from as he leads. While Americans are used to religious insincerity from their political leaders, Obama seems to be sincere in what he proclaims. He embraced religion long before he embraced politics. Indeed, it was his faith that gave him the will to serve in public office, and the worldview of that faith that shaped his understanding of what he would do once he came to power.

Here there is an important distinction. There have been other Democrats who were religiously fluent, of course. Bill Clinton and Jimmy Carter come to mind. Yet both men seemed to truncate their faith, to even erect a wall of separation between faith and practice. Obama's faith infuses his public policy, so that his faith is not just limited to the personal realms of his life; it also informs his leadership. One can imagine, in an Obama presidency, White House conferences on Faith and Poverty or Religion's Response to Racism that are more than theater, more than time wasting mockeries of national ills. Obama roots his political Liberalism in a theological worldview, and he will call others to do the same, much to the challenge of what has come before: the secular Left, the truncated faith of traditional politics, certainly, the now-fading Religious Right.

Yet Obama seems willing to join with those of differing faiths to solve the crises of his times, to tend the wounds of his nation. Here, too, there may be an opportunity to heal, whoever wins the presidency in 2008. Perhaps we have come to a moment when a common devotion to God may fuel a national resolve to break cycles of poverty, challenge strongholds of racism, reinforce ethical conduct among the powerful and the powerless, deliberate on the morality of war before it is declared, and end the moral scourges of our time. If this is so, then part of the impact of Barack Obama in our generation may be for just such a purpose: to help wed faith to a political vision that leads to meaningful change in our time.

Acknowledgments

IT WAS MY SOUTHERN GRANDMOTHER WHO ONCE CHARGED me to "never speak of religion or politics in polite company." She may have been right, though I have done little else ever since. Still, her counsel was not lost on me, for I realized even those many years ago that she was urging me toward a gentler manner with others, one of graciousness and consideration rather than the sharp and divisive way. She was trying to bring the South to bear on her brash, military-brat grandson, and how often I have wished that her tradition lived more nobly in my soul. Because it does not, I have at least had the wisdom to gather about me greater minds and loftier spirits than I will ever be.

Chief among them is my wife, Beverly. Always my first counsel, first editor, and first comfort in a writer's despair, she is that unique combination of lover and coach, champion and loyal opposition, which makes me better than I naturally am. What she does for my writing she also does for my life, transforming both by her passion, her joy, and her strength.

The firm she leads, Chartwell Literary Group (www.chartwell-literary.com), is a team of literary experts I cannot live without. It is their sense of a book's spirit, of the creative possibilities of the printed word, that inspires me and helps me see the wonder of books as though for the first time. Under Beverly's wise guidance, Chartwell is becoming a writer's band of brothers and the answer to a publisher's prayer.

Joining her on my immediate team has been Dr. George Grant—older brother, mentor, and friend—who allowed me in this book to critique the very Religious Right he has loved, pastored, chastised, and intellectually led. His graciousness in the face of my views and his patience in the face of my demands on his time are evidence of a character I can only hope to emulate.

Melinda Gales of the Gales Network (www.galesnetwork.com) scheduled the interviews that made this book what it is, while her husband, David, helped me understand the manuscript through his kind but unsparing eyes. Michaela Jackson, research genius and editor, never ceased to remind me that her generation—the young who "do faith like jazz"—cannot be ignored in the Obama story, and I trust that I have captured both the passion and the importance of that tribe in this book. Dimples Kellogg so skillfully edited the manuscript that she left me wondering if I have ever written anything in the true English language. Dan Williamson, David Holland, and Stephen Prather have given wise counsel, and I am grateful to each of these, but for their friendship most of all.

There have been many generous souls willing to speak with us about the themes that touch Barack Obama's life. Jim Wallis of Sojourners helped me understand the cause of social justice and Obama's commitment to it in a lengthy interview that I will always recall with gratitude. Dr. Dwight N. Hopkins of the University of

Chicago Divinity School graciously read my treatment of black theology and Jeremiah Wright, taking time to gently help this white man understand. Ambassador Alan Keyes offered his characteristic fire in recounting the Illinois Senate race of 2004, and George Barna showed us why he is one of the true wise men of our age. Professor Paul Kengor of Grove City College offered us insight beyond his seminal *God and Hillary Clinton: A Spiritual Life*, and Guy Rodgers, once national director of Americans of Faith for McCain, helped us understand the man he has served so well. Dr. Jeff Clark, of both Middle Tennessee State University and McLean/ Clark in Washington, D.C., gave us keen understanding of who Obama is, and Dave Zinati provided unique insight into the reality of the Religious Right.

I must also thank Trinity United Church of Christ for hosting me so graciously over an Easter weekend, Archbishop Desmond Tutu for his encouraging words, and Malcolm DuPlessis for bringing the Archbishop into our lives.

Joel Miller, Episcopal comrade in arms, has made working with Thomas Nelson a joy, and Esther Fedorkevich, agent and friend, has made this book possible by tending the thousand and one details that allowed me to write. Strategic support of an essential kind has been provided by Jim Laffoon, Brett Fuller, Sam Webb, and Norman Nakanishi. They are friends and fathers, all, and I could not do without them.

Finally, deepest appreciation to the Obama campaign staff for fielding our many inquiries and requests for interviews. Their dream of meaningful change is certainly evident in the way they received us, and we are grateful beyond words.

Notes

Introduction

1. Todd Purdum, "Raising Obama," *Vanity Fair,* March 2008.
2. The Barna Group, "Born Again Voters No Longer Favor Republican Candidates," February 4, 2008, 1, http://www.barna.org/FlexPage.aspx?Page=BarnaUpdateNarrow&BarnaUpdateID=291.
3. Adam Nagourney and Megan Thee, "Young Americans Are Leaning Left, New Poll Finds," *New York Times,* June 27, 2007.
4. Steve Dougherty, *Hopes and Dreams: The Story of Barack Obama* (New York: Black Dog and Leventhal Publishers, 2007), 9.

Chapter 1—To Walk Between Two Worlds

1. Janny Scott, "The Long Run: In 2000, a Streetwise Veteran Schooled a Bold Young Obama," *New York Times,* September 9, 2007.
2. Barack Obama, *Dreams from My Father* (New York: Three Rivers Press, 1995), 15.
3. Tim Jones, "Special Report: Making of a Candidate," *Chicago Tribune,* March 27, 2007.
4. Ibid.
5. Obama, *Dreams,* 17.
6. Jones, "Special Report."
7. Paul Johnson, *Modern Times* (New York: HarperCollins, 1983), 479.
8. Ibid.
9. Obama, *Dreams,* 50.

10. Barack Obama, *The Audacity of Hope* (New York: Three Rivers Press, 2006), 204.

11. Abul Ala Maudidi, *The Punishment of the Apostate According to Islamic Law* (Lahore: Islamic Publications, 1994), 30–31.

12. Obama, *Dreams*, 58.

13. Ibid., 86.

14. Purdum, "Raising Obama."

15. Sharon Cohen, "Barack Obama Straddles Different Worlds," *USA Today,* December 14, 2007.

16. Obama, *Dreams*, xv.

17. Ibid., 155.

18. Obama, *Audacity*, 206.

19. Obama, *Dreams*, 287.

20. Obama, *Audacity*, 209.

21. Ibid., 208.

CHAPTER 2—MY HOUSE, TOO

1. Tim Grieve, "Left Turn at Saddleback Church," Salon.com, December 2, 2006.

2. Iva E. Carruthers, Frederick D. Haynes II, and Jeremiah A. Wright Jr., eds., *Blow the Trumpet in Zion* (Minneapolis: Fortress Press, 2005), 5.

3. Ibid.

4. Ibid.

5. Ibid., 6.

6. Ibid., 5.

7. Manya A. Brachear, "Rev. Jeremiah A. Wright, Jr.: Pastor Inspires Obama's 'Audacity,'" *Chicago Tribune,* January 21, 2007.

8. Luke 4:18 NIV

9. James H. Cone, *A Black Theology of Liberation: Twentieth Anniversary Edition,* (New York: Orbis, 1986), 45–46.

10. James H. Cone, *God of the Oppressed* (New York: Orbis, 1997), xi.

11. Cone, *A Black Theology of Liberation*, 38.

12. Ibid., 35.

13. Ibid., 28.

14. Ibid., 25.
15. William A. Von Hoene Jr., "Rev. Wright in a Different Light," *Chicago Tribune*, March 26, 2008.

CHAPTER 3—FAITH FIT FOR THE AGE

1. Obama, *Audacity*, 208.
2. Cathleen Falsani, "I Have a Deep Faith," *Chicago Sun Times*, April 5, 2005; Sarah Pulliam and Ted Olson, "Q&A: Barack Obama," *Christianity Today*, January 2008, Web-only edition, http://www.christianitytoday.com/ct/2008/januaryweb-only/104-32.0.html.
3. Obama, *Audacity*, 208.
4. Barack Obama, "Call to Renewal" Keynote Address, Wednesday, June 28, 2006, Washington, D.C.
5. Obama, *Audacity*, 206.
6. Ibid., 208.
7. Ibid.
8. Ibid.
9. John K. Wilson, *Barack Obama: This Improbable Quest* (Boulder: Paradigm Publishers, 2008), 136.
10. Ibid., 137.
11. Ibid., 138.
12. Ibid.
13. Obama, "Call to Renewal."
14. Falsani, "I Have a Deep Faith."
15. Obama, *Audacity*, 204.
16. Falsani, "I Have a Deep Faith."
17. Wilson, 138.
18. Obama, *Audacity*, 226.
19. Wilson, 139.
20. Ibid.
21. Falsani, "I Have a Deep Faith."
22. Obama, *Audacity*, 222.
23. 2 Tim. 3:16 KJV

24. Ibid., 224.

25. Barack Obama, "On My Faith and My Church," March 14, 2008, http://www.realclearpolitics.com/articles/2008/03/on_my_faith_and_my_church.html.

26. Author's interview with Jim Wallis, April 8, 2008.

Chapter 4—Our Civic Religion

1. The details of this vignette are based on the description of Abraham Lincoln's congressional race against Rev. Peter Cartwright in Carl Sandburg's *Abraham Lincoln: The Prairie Years and the War Years* (New York: Harcourt, Brace & World, Inc., 1954), 83–84.

2. Obama, *Audacity*, 46–47.

3. Ibid., 18.

4. David Mendell, *Obama: From Promise to Power* (New York: Amistad, 2007), 261.

5. Race 4 2008, "Alan Keyes," http://race42008.com/alan-keyes.

6. Obama, *Audacity*, 209.

7. Ibid., 210.

8. John Chase and Liam Ford, "Senate Debate Gets Personal," *Chicago Tribune*, October 22, 2004.

9. Liam Ford and David Mendell, "Jesus Wouldn't Vote for Obama, Keyes Says," *Chicago Tribune*, September 8, 2004.

10. Ibid.

11. Ibid.

12. Ibid.

13. Obama, *Audacity*, 211.

14. "Call to Renewal."

15. Ibid.

16. The speech served as the rough draft for the chapter on faith in Obama's *The Audacity of Hope*, published the same year.

17. E. J. Dionne, Op-Ed., *Washington Post*, June 30, 2006.

18. Peter Wood, "Obama's Prayer: Wooing Evangelicas," *National Review*, July 6, 2006, http://article.nationalreview.com?q=ZTMzNDU5ZDU4Zjhi YTkxMzhhNTk3Y2M5MmRhMmJkY2U=.

19. A compilation from Hegel by Karl R. Popper, *The Open Society and Its Enemies*, 4th ed., 2 vols. (Princeton: Princeton University Press, 1963), 2:31.

20. Falsani, "I Have a Deep Faith."

21. Will Herberg, *Catholic-Protestant-Jew*, rev. ed. (Garden City, NY: Doubleday Anchor, 1960), 260.

22. Herbert Schlossberg, *Idols for Destruction* (Nashville: Thomas Nelson, 1983), 252.

23. Ibid., 251.

24. Pulliam and Olsen, "Q&A: Barack Obama."

25. Amanda B. Carpenter, "Obama More Pro-Choice Than NARAL," *Human Events*, December 25, 2006, http://www.humanevents.com/article.php?id=18647.

26. NARAL release, 6/13, as quoted in "Opinion | NARAL Says It Does Not Oppose Born Alive Infants Act, Calls Bill 'Trap' to Put Abortion-Rights Supporters on Defensive" in Kaiser Daily Women's Health Policy section, Daily Reports, June 20, 2001, http://www.kaisernetwork.org/daily_reports/rep_index.cfm?DR_ID=5334.

27. Carpenter, "Obama More Pro-Choice Than NARAL."

28. Ibid.

29. Obama, *Audacity*, 223–24.

CHAPTER 5—FOUR FACES OF FAITH

1. McCain and Salter, 71.

2. Ibid., 152.

3. John Arundel, "Episcopal Fetes a Favorite Son," *Alexandria Times*, December 6, 2007.

4. McCain and Salter, 329.

5. Ibid., 332.

6. Ibid., 223.

7. Ibid., 286.

8. Terry Mattingly, "George W. Bush Learns to 'Testify'," Scripps Howard News Service, March 17, 1999, http://tmatt.gospelcom.net/column/1999/03/17/.

9. Hillary Rodham Clinton, *It Takes a Village* (New York: Simon & Schuster, 1996), 171.

10. Paul Kengor, *God and Hillary Clinton: A Spiritual Life* (New York: HarperCollins, 2007), 16.

11. Ibid., 72.

12. Kenneth L. Woodward, "Soulful Matters," *Newsweek*, October 31, 1994.

13. Ibid.

14. Bob Woodward, *The Choice* (New York: Simon and Schuster, 1996), 130–32.

15. Kengor, 155.

16. Ibid.

17. Michael Luo, "Faith Intertwines with Political Life for Clinton," *The New York Times*, July 7, 2007.

18. Obama, *Audacity*, quoted in Kenneth T. Walsh, "Talkin' 'Bout My Generation," *U.S. News & World Report*, December 31, 2006, http://www.usnews.com/usnews/news/articles/061231/8obama.htm.

19. Stephen Mansfield, "How the President Found God," *Charisma* magazine, October 2003, http://www.charismamag.com/display.php?id=8075&print=yes.

20. Gail Sheehy, "The Accidental Candidate," *Vanity Fair*, October 2000, 174.

21. Sam Howe-Verhovek, "Is There Room on the Republican Ticket for Another Bush?" *New York Times Magazine*, September 13, 1998.

22. The account of the meeting between Bush, Blessitt, and Sale was taken from Arthur Blessitt's Web site (http://www.blessitt.com/bush.html) and was corroborated and further developed by the author's interviews with Blessitt on June 30, 2003 and Jim Sale on June 17, 2003.

23. Skip Hollandsworth, "Younger, Wilder," *Texas Monthly Report*, June 1999.

24. Tony Carnes, "A Presidential Hopeful's Progress," *Christianity Today*, October 2, 2000.

25. Ibid.

26. David Frum, *The Right Man: The Surprise Presidency of George W. Bush* (New York: Random House, 2003), 283.

27. James Robison, interview with author, tape recording, Dallas, Texas, May 28, 2003. The conversation between Robison and Bush was first recorded in the author's *The Faith of George W. Bush* (New York: Penguin, 1983).

28. Ibid.

29. Barack Obama, comments prepared for delivery before the national meeting of the United Church of Christ, quoted in Stephen Singer, "Obama Says Some Have Hijacked Faith," http://www.breitbart.com/article.php?id=D8PUN7AO0&show_article=1&cat=0.

CHAPTER 6—A TIME TO HEAL

1. Abraham Lincoln, Second Inaugural Address, March 4, 1865.

2. Richard Norton Smith, *Eulogy for President Ford*, January 3, 2007.

3. William Shakespeare, *Julius Caesar*, act 4, scene 3.

4. George Will, *Nashville Banner*, January 25, 1993.

5. George Will, *Washington Post*, July 5, 1990.

6. Michael Drummond, *Participatory Democracy: A New Federalism in the Making* (New York: L. T. Carnell and Sons, 1923), 22.

7. Jeremiah Wright, National Press Club speech, April 28, 2008. These comments can be heard, in part, online at http://www.breitbart.tv/?p=85643.

8. Bill Clinton, May 16, 1997, transcript titled "Clinton Apologizes for Tuskegee," http://www.npr.org/transcripts.

9. Ibid.

10. Martin Luther King Jr., "A Knock at Midnight," in *A Knock at Midnight: Inspiration from the Great Sermons of Reverend Martin Luther King, Jr.* (New York: Grand Central Publishing, 2000), 72–73.

11. Barack Obama, "A More Perfect Union," March 18, 2008.

12. Ibid.

13. Ibid.

14. Otis Moss III, quoted in Manya A. Brachear, "Speech Parallels a Transition at Trinity Church," *Chicago Tribune*, March 19, 2008, http://www.chicagotribune.com/news/chi-obama-wright-churchmar19,1,4714248.story.

15. Ibid.

16. Nancy Gibbs and Michael Duffy, "How the Democrats Got Religion," *Time*, July 12, 2007.

17. Ibid.

18. Ibid.
19. Ibid.

Bibliography

Anyabwile, Thabiti M. *The Decline of African American Theology: From Biblical Faith to Cultural Captivity.* Downers Grove, IL: Academic, 2007.

Barna, George and Harry R. Jackson Jr. *High Impact African-American Churches.* Ventura, CA: Regal, 2008.

Carruthers, Iva E., Frederick D. Haynes III, and Jeremiah A. Wright Jr., eds. *Blow the Trumpet in Zion: Global Vision and Action for the 21st Century Black Church.* Minneapolis: Fortress Press, 2005.

Cone, James H. *Risks of Faith: The Emergence of Black Theology of Liberation, 1968-1998.* Boston: Beacon Press, 1999.

———. *A Black Theology of Liberation: Twentieth Anniversary Edition.* Maryknoll, NY: Orbis Books, 1986.

Dougherty, Steve. *Hopes and Dreams: The Story of Barack Obama.* New York: Black Dog and Leventhal Publishers, 2007.

Kengor, Paul. *God and Hillary Clinton: A Spiritual Life.* New York: HarperCollins, 2007.

McCain, John and Mark Salter. *Faith of My Fathers: A Family Memoir.* New York: Random House, 1999.

Mansfield, Stephen. *The Faith of George W. Bush.* New York: Penguin, 2003.

Mendell, David. *Obama: From Promise to Power.* New York: Amistad, 2007.

Obama, Barack. *The Audacity of Hope: Thoughts on Reclaiming the American Dream.* New York: Three Rivers Press, 2006.

———. *Dreams from My Father: A Story of Race and Inheritance.* New York: Three Rivers Press, 1995.

Steele, Shelby. *A Bound Man: Why We Are Excited About Obama and Why He Can't Win.* New York: Free Press, 2008.

Wallis, Jim. *The Great Awakening: Reviving Faith & Politics in a Post-Religious Right America.* New York: HarperCollins, 2008.

Wilson, John K. *Barack Obama: This Improbable Quest.* Boulder: Paradigm, 2007.

About the Author

STEPHEN MANSFIELD IS THE *NEW YORK TIMES* BEST-SELLING author of *The Faith of George W. Bush, The Faith of the American Soldier, Then Darkness Fled: The Liberating Wisdom of Booker T. Washington,* and *Never Give In: The Extraordinary Character of Winston Churchill,* among other works of history and biography. Founder of both The Mansfield Group, a research and communications firm, and Chartwell Literary Group, which creates and manages literary projects, Stephen is also in wide demand as a lecturer and inspirational speaker. For more information, log on to www.mansfieldgroup.com.

Index

Numbers in *italic* indicate pages with illustrations